# Pole Power

Changing the Face of Poland's Energy
for the European Union

## Richard Mersey

Talleyrand Books

Published by Talleyrand Books
PO Box 2073
Pulborough
RH20 1YA

A CIP catalogue record for this book is available from the British Library.

ISBN 1 902320 23 9

Printed in Great Britain.


Richard Mersey would like to thank the Polonia Aid Foundation Trust for sponsoring the publication of this book.

To Alan Stretton

# Glossary

| | |
|---|---|
| BCM | Billion Cubic Metres |
| BNFL | British Nuclear Fuels Ltd, Sellafield |
| CCGT | Combined Cycle Gas Turbine |
| CHP | Combined Heat and Power |
| $CO_2$ | Carbon dioxide |
| DM | Deutschmarks |
| DTI | Department of Trade and Industry |
| EBRD | European Bank for Reconstruction and Development |
| ERA | Energy Regulatory Authority |
| FGD | Flue Gas Desulphurisation |
| GDP | Gross Domestic Product |
| GW (E) | Gigawatts (Electric). One gigawatt is one thousand megawatts. |
| Huta | Polish for steel. |
| IGCC | Integrated Gasification Combined Cycle |
| IPPC | Integrated prevention of pollution control |
| KV | One thousand volts. |
| KW | One thousand watts. (e.g. a one bar electric fire.) |
| LCPD | The large combustion plant directive |
| MOX | Mixed Oxide Nuclear fuel. |
| MTOE | Million tonnes of oil equivalent. |
| MWE | A million watts of electricity. |
| MWT | A million watts thermal. |
| NATO | North Atlantic Treaty Organisation |
| NOX | Nitrous Oxide |
| OECD | Organisation for Economic Co-operation and Development |
| PFB | Pressurised fluidised bed. |

| | |
|---|---|
| PHARE | The EU's main funding channel for acceding Countries |
| POGC | The Polish Oil and Gas Company |
| PSE | The Polish National Grid |
| REC | Regional Electricity Company |
| RJB | Richard Budge Mining Ltd. |
| Sejm, The | The lower and stronger of the two Polish Houses of Parliament. |
| $SO_2$ | Sulphur dioxide |
| TPA | Third Party Access |
| Voivod | The head of a voivodship. |
| Voivodship | A Region of Poland: e.g. Silesia. There are 15 voivodships in Poland. Below them are smaller units, Powiats, and below them again Gminas. |
| Wegiel | Polish for coal. |
| Zloty | The unit of Polish currency. Abbreviated it is pln (around 7 to the £). |

# Contents

|  |  | Page |
|---|---|---|
| Foreword |  | 9 |
| Introduction |  | 11 |
| Chapter 1 | Poland in the Twentieth Century: The Communists | 15 |
| Chapter 2 | Unsaddling the Socialist Cow | 28 |
| Chapter 3 | Black Gold: Poland's Fuel | 40 |
| Chapter 4 | Coal Exports | 61 |
| Chapter 5 | Coal for Heat | 67 |
| Chapter 6 | Gas | 73 |
| Chapter 7 | The Lignite Story | 88 |
| Chapter 8 | Hard Coal and Electricity | 97 |
| Chapter 9 | The National Grid (PSE) and the Sale of Electricity | 110 |
| Chapter 10 | The Polish Environment | 119 |
| Chapter 11 | Polish and United Kingdom's Energy Compared | 135 |
| Chapter 12 | Polish and German Energy Compared | 145 |
| Chapter 13 | Poland's Transition Towards the EU | 160 |
| Chapter 14 | The *Acquis* (I): Energy | 171 |
|  | The *Acquis* (II): General | 176 |
| Chapter 15 | The *Acquis* and the Environment | 182 |
| Chapter 16 | The future of Polish Energy | 193 |
| Postscript |  | 198 |
| Acknowledgements |  | 201 |
| Index |  | 206 |

# Foreword

At the Congress of Vienna in 1815 Charles Maurice de Talleyrand Perigord, representing France, held the view that the partition of Poland had been a crime and that its reconstruction was desirable.

'The re-establishment of the Kingdom of Poland would be a benefit and a very great benefit but only on the three following conditions:
1. That it should be independent
2. That it should have a strong Constitution
3. That it should not be necessary to compensate Prussia and Austria for the parts they would lose.'

Talleyrand continued that it was impossible to fulfil these conditions and that partition must continue. But it should only be temporary.

'By remaining partitioned Poland will not be destroyed for ever. The Poles although not forming a political entity will always form a family. They will no longer have a common country but they will have a common language. They will therefore remain united by the strongest and most lasting of all bonds. They will, under foreign domination, reach the age of manhood which they have not achieved in nine centuries of independence., and the moment when they reach it will not be far distant from the moment when, having won their freedom, they will rally round one centre.'

The future that Talleyrand foresaw was accomplished briefly between the two world wars. Then Poland was invaded by Hitler and later annexed by Stalin.

Only with the collapse of the Soviet Union in 1989 has Talleyrand's dream become a reality.

Today's independent Poland looks towards full scale membership of the European Union.

# INTRODUCTION

## Poland, Energy and Environment

Poland is the largest of the six countries seeking admission to the EU in the next tranche.

There are many barriers to her accession. I will concentrate on that barrier caused by her power sector and the pollution it causes.

Of the six candidates for entry, Poland is uniquely dependent on coal for power. The coal and the power pollute Poland's land, rivers and air.

A good starting point is to examine the state of Poland's environment in the key year of 1989, the year of the fall of the Soviet Union.

To show the scale of the problem I will examine her environment in all its aspects under the Communists.

The data is sketchy. Emissions from farms, hospitals, recreation centres and workshops were not monitored. Small plants were not covered at all. Regular monitoring took place only in the 1,362 'particularly harmful' plants, and they total a mere 10% of known sources of toxic emissions. Not withstanding these limitations, the data paint 'A bleak picture in air and water pollution and abatement, soil degradation and contamination, industrial and municipal waste discharge, deforestation, landscape protection, land use and protection of fauna and flora' (George Blazyca and Ryszard Rapacki, *Poland into the 90s*, Pinter, 1991).

Poland was without doubt one of the most heavily polluted countries in Europe. The extent of pollution differed regionally. The government identified 27 ecologically threatened areas covering 11% of the country but 35% of the population. In these areas the ecological balance was totally disrupted and health hazards were considerable.

In these threatened areas, populated by 380 people per square km, there occurred:

61% of industrial and municipal effluent.

58% of non-treated waste water.

75% of dust emission.

80% of gaseous pollutants.

Some 93% of total waste was deposited there, which is 40 tonnes per square km.

The Communist Government had environmental norms, which were in excess of those obtaining in Western Europe. Even so those living in Silesia in particular were exposed to pollution levels far exceeding those officially allowed. For instance:

Dust particles in the air: 40 times the allowable norm.

Nitrogen oxides: 7 times.

Carbon monoxide: 50 times.

Lead and benzo-a-piren: 60 times.

In the area around Katowice, Silesia's main conurbation which covers around 2% of Poland's territory, the population density is 5 times higher than average. Located there were 4,000 big and medium-sized enterprises. Among them could be found one quarter of Poland's most serious polluters.

In general there was:

1. Accelerated forest decline due to insufficient control of noxious pollutants such as sulphur dioxide ($SO_2$).

2. Growth of municipal and industrial wastes deposited in the environment.

3. Degradation of water resources in rural areas and concomitant worsening of sanitation in the countryside.

**Atmospheric Pollution**

60 to 70% of total air pollution originated in power stations, chemical plants and in the metallurgy and building materials industries. Only 10 to 15% came from transport.

In 1988 Polish industry and power generation discharged 5.2 million tonnes of gaseous pollutant into the air, including 2.8 million tonnes of sulphur dioxide, 1.4 million tonnes of carbon monoxide and 0.8 million tonnes of nitrogen oxides.

The dismal catalogue continues; regarding heavy metals, Poland emitted excessive quantities of cadmium, mercury and lead. The emission of all atmospheric pollutants had been growing for many years with sulphur dioxide the worst offender.

**Water Pollution**

Half the industrial plants had no purification facilities. 110 towns had no sewage system. 374 towns did not treat their sewage. Most rural sewage was discharged untreated to surface water, and water quality was worsened further by the run off from pesticides and fertilisers.

Of Poland's total river length where water quality was monitored, only 4.2% was described as first class. 40% of it was below any standard and unsuitable for any economic use.

The poor quality of surface waters degraded the marine environment of the Baltic.

Pollution of ground water had also been increasing and this was more disturbing because it was used for drinking.

**Land Use and Waste Disposal**

At the end of 1988, 100,000 hectares of land were devastated and degraded. Of that only 4% was re-cultivated. 186 million tonnes of industrial waste was generated. Just under half of it was deposited in permanent storage sites. This gave Poland an accumulated volume of 1.5 billion tonnes.

**Forests**

Forests cover 27.7% of Poland's territory. In 1987 only 24.4% of coniferous forest and 46.6% of deciduous forest was undamaged.

This sad list shows the vast scale of the environmental problem in Poland as the Communists fell from power.

Poland's first freely elected Government published an Outline Economic Programme in October 1989 which was rather optimistic. It claimed that, 'the switch to the market economy will force out energy and raw material gobbling technologies... first, thanks to modernization of the economic structure, devastation of the environment will be reduced. Second, a State which no longer has to administer directly to the economy can pursue a more effective ecological policy. Protection of the environment will be an integral element of the economic system and enterprises will face the real cost of using natural resources.'

# CHAPTER 1

## Poland in the Twentieth Century:
## The Communists

Before the Second World War Poland had an agricultural economy. She was one of the new countries formed at the Treaty of Versailles. She called herself 'The Second Republic'.

The first republic was a creature of the sixteenth century. Then, Poland stretched from the Baltic to the Black Sea. This hugely powerful Empire was surrounded by the three aggressive powers of Austria, Prussia and Russia. Slowly, these chipped away at the Polish Empire until, by 1795, there was nothing left of it. It was partitioned between the three invaders.

The curious Second Republic lasted for less than twenty years. Some of its boundaries had been decided by plebiscite, and quite possibly had been rigged. A Polish corridor was driven through Germany to isolate East Prussia. Danzig, German speaking, headed this corridor and was declared a Free City. Further east, the Poles invaded Russia in 1922 and included in their new country parts of Belorus and the Ukraine. She thus had considerable eastern territories that were not ethnically Polish. Russians, Lats, Ruthenians and Gypsies also lived there.

This Republic was predominantly a land of peasant farmers, a tradition continuing to an extent even today, with 25% of the Poles working on the land and the average farm size seven hectares. The country was particularly primitive in the east, where there were few roads or railways.

Yet Poland has always seen herself as a West European power.

She admired the British parliamentary system. She found common cause with the French Revolutionaries.

But each time the Poles have turned to the West for help we have let them down: seven times since 1772.

The Second Republic ended with the Nazi invasion of 1939, triggering World War II, as there was in place the Anglo French Polish Alliance. This stated that an attack on Poland constituted an attack on all three countries. What is a little less well known is that the Polish fulfilled their part of the bargain, which was to hold up the German Army for two weeks. Seventy French Divisions would then plunge over the Maginot line into Germany. The only Allied material that actually plunged into Germany was a few thousand leaflets. Meanwhile, the Polish Army managed to hold on for six weeks. They actually lasted longer than the French Army in 1940. And they were fighting Russia as well as Germany.

After the war Poland looked hopefully West again. But the die had been cast at Yalta and Poland was destined to become a Russian satellite. Poland's leader, Gomulka, was a true independent Communist, like Tito, and Poland could have quite possibly become a second Yugoslavia if she had been on the Mediterranean, not the Baltic. Indeed, Stalin might almost have been relieved had this happened, as he likened ruling the Poles to trying to put a saddle on a cow: a peculiarly apt remark since he never managed to get rid of Poland's peasant farmers.

There were bigger issues at stake. Stalin was still frightened of Germany, as indeed was Winston Churchill. To form a buttress against the Germans Poland must industrialise. She must become a Russian colony supplying the mother country with steel for tanks and guns.

To show Russian dominance over Poland, the highest building in the new Warsaw was to be the Russian Palace of Culture. Strangely the highest building in old Warsaw had been the Russian Alexander Nevski Cathedral built by the Czars. *Plus ça change.*

A bigger example of Russian dominance rose around Krakow. This medieval city in the former Austrian zone had been untouched by war. It was Poland's academic capital. Stalin built to its east a huge aluminium smelter, and to its west an entire new town and factory, Nowa Huta (i.e., New Steel Works). The result was the worst pollution I have ever seen. Krakow lies in a bowl, so all particulate emissions from the works and the power stations supplying them fell into it. By 1997, when I was first in Krakow, the aluminium smelter had closed down and the steel works was working at a quarter capacity so the air was fairly clean. However, I saw a conservator chipping away at deposits on a stained glass window in the cathedral. It looked as if it had been blacked out against the Luftwaffe.

In the 1970s the Russians built an even bigger steelworks 40 miles to the west: Huta Katowice.

Communists believed that the industrial worker was superior to the peasant. That accounts for the industrialisation of all of Eastern Europe after the Second World War, and the consequent need for much more energy. The need for more power was ubiquitous but the fuel used to create it varied: nuclear, gas, oil, or, as in Poland's case, coal.

Poland's boundaries changed after the Second World War. The whole country shifted westward. She lost her eastern territories, which was no great catastrophe as they were amongst her poorest and were in any event not ethnically Polish. She gained

German territory as far west as the rivers Oder and Neisse. The Germans in these territories were mostly deported back to East Germany as, obviously, Germans were not welcome in Poland after the destruction of Warsaw and the creation of Auschwitz, Treblinka and other horrors.

The most significant Polish gain in the West was the whole of Silesia. This contains a considerable coalfield. Before the Second World War it was split between Germany and Poland. Now it is entirely Polish and very big. Even today Poland remains the seventh largest coal producer in the world.

Thus Poland's energy sector was to increase steadily over the next 40 years for two reasons.

Firstly, it was general Communist policy to favour industry. Secondly, Poland had unrivalled quantities of coal with which that industry could be fuelled.

There are only 66 deep coal-mines in Silesia, but each mine is ten or even twenty times the size of, say, a British mine or a Ruhr mine. The seams are wide and level. It was these attractions that caused the work force of miners to rise to half a million. They left the poverty of their farms and came to Silesia from all parts of Poland. Silesia's population rose to seven million. Miners were well paid.

It must have been deliberate Russian policy to make Poland's power almost wholly reliant on coal. The Poles were not pressured into building nuclear power stations as were Hungary, Bulgaria and Lithuania. Russian natural gas pipelines were all routed south of Poland, via the Ukraine and Czechoslovakia.

It is also true that the Poles themselves preferred coal, as it was their own. They surely did not wish to be dependent on their huge eastern neighbour, so prone to invade them over the centuries. Besides, they could export coal to the West. Throughout the period of Russian occupation, coal was Poland's biggest earner of hard currency.

The Poles were also forced to supply the Soviet Union with coal, which was a positive disadvantage since they were not paid for it. But four times as much coal went west as went east.

Two words common enough in the West do not have much meaning in a Soviet style economy. They are 'cost' and 'pollution'. In a command economy, costs are normally not known and may even be irrelevant. The coal-mines did not keep profit and loss accounts. They were not separate entities. They were simply part of the Ministry of Mines. To ask, in Communist days, 'Is Halemba mine profitable?' is not so much an unanswerable question as a non-question. The miners had one goal only. That was to produce more coal each year.

As for 'pollution', a true Stalinist might regard this word as symptomatic of the degenerate West. Communists are tough. Communists are men of steel. They are not concerned over inhaling a bit of soot or sulphur dioxide. Incidentally, I have yet to meet a Russian who puts the Chernobyl death rate any higher than '36 brave firemen'. It is quite hard to refute this figure.

With hindsight, it is obvious that Poland has been busy making her entry into the EU more environmentally difficult over the period 1945 to 1989. She has constructed an expensive polluting industry of which she is now trying to rid herself.

England started to construct such an industry at the end of the 18th century. It seems odd that the Soviet Bloc did not recognise the problems raised 200 years earlier. I understood that Soviet schoolchildren were taught that dark Satanic mills were typical of the capitalist West and that the filth of Dickensian London was typical of London today. But then of course not many children believed what they were taught.

The coal-mines themselves pollute water more than air. The coal is fairly low in sulphur, but high in salt. This must be washed out, and the process pollutes the rivers, in particular the Vistula, to the extent that it is actually more saline than the Baltic Sea.

It is the power stations that pollute the air. Poland still has the capacity to generate 30 gigawatts of electricity. Pre 1989 this would all have been used and the flue gases would have been discharged into the atmosphere untreated. The centre of pollution is the Katowice conurbation. It is a fairly clean area now, but the evidence of the old filth can be seen all around in the blackest buildings that I have ever come across.

It is quite hard for a twenty-first century Westerner to grasp the concept that heavy industrial growth is an end in itself. True, this was so in nineteenth century England, but the motive was profit. The sort of directive that it is hard to understand is that the solution to a surplus of steel is to decree that all new bed frames be made twice as heavy. It is much easier to respond to a surplus of steel by eliminating that surplus, but that might cause unemployment, which does not exist in Soviet society, so if reduction is not an option one does end up logically with a steel bed that one cannot lift.

As with steel, so with power. Up to 1989 the head of each power station aimed to produce more power than the year before, for that was how his success was measured. That this caused power to be wasted is obvious, but since it was not priced it did not really matter.

It is offensive to Westerners to see a district heating system leaking at every joint, and to learn that the water in the system is so corrosive that neither valves nor thermostats can be fitted, and the only way, therefore, for the householder to regulate heat is by opening the window.

I suggest that words like 'waste', 'economical' and 'thrift' do not mean anything in a command economy.

\* \* \*

1989 must surely go down as the great watershed year of the millennium. Exactly two hundred years earlier a dictatorial monarchy had been overthrown in France. But 1989 marked the collapse of the greatest territorial empire that the world has ever seen. That year saw the Poles at the gates of Elysium, or so they thought. In fact Western capitalism is not a bed of roses and the Poles were to have the shock of their lives, along with all the other 'satellites' or colonies of the former Soviet Union. Eastern Europe was quite unprepared for the fundamental change in thinking needed to make the transition from command economy (Communism) to market economy (capitalism).

So before taking the story forward I would like to delve back to highlight a few features contributing to the Polish mindset of 1989.

The Poles had been extraordinarily skilful in avoiding direct Russian intervention. Both Hungary and Czechoslovakia had gone too fast too far in 1956 and 1968. The Poles had always managed to be just disruptive enough to annoy without causing a Russian invasion.

The two great leaders of the period were Gomulka and Gierek. I think it fair to describe them as genuine Communist leaders who did not wish to kow-tow to Russia, yet who realised also that politics is the art of the possible. There was never outright rebellion. But there were strikes, civil unrest and riots. These were in a different league from those of the United Kingdom in the same period. A few thousand Poles were actually shot, and ten times more imprisoned.

In August 1980 increases in food prices ignited strikes in the shipyards which spread to steelworks and coalmines. The Solidarity Union, led by Lech Walesa, emerged as a popular national protest movement and soon had 10 million members.

In the Gdansk agreement of 31 August 1980 Walesa secured the following concessions:

1. The right to strike.
2. Increased wages.
3. Public broadcasts of Sunday Mass.
4. Relaxation of censorship.
5. Reform of welfare provisions.
6. Managers selected by ability, not party affiliation.
7. An overhaul of the entire economic system by consulting the independent trade unions.

In truth 1980 did mark the beginning of the end for the Russians. Other factors made it so as well as Walesa himself.

Two years earlier, Cardinal Karol Wojtyla had been elected Pope. This evoked the true Poland: an ancient Catholic nation, besides which Communism was no more than a passing phenomenon. Next, the Russians actually allowed the Pope to visit his homeland. Anyone who has seen film of the Pope and his massed congregations in Krakow and Zakopane would find these quite incompatible with a godless Communist system. Gorbachev himself believed that Communism was finished in Poland once the Holy Father had set foot in his native country.

Thirdly, there was satellite television. It was no longer possible to fool Eastern Europe that the Communist system was the best when its people could see with their own eyes the material advantages of capitalism. There are those, including the former Director General of the BBC John Birt, who attribute the collapse of the Communist system entirely to television.

However, whether caused by the Pope, Walesa or TV the 1980 uprising failed to free Poland. Russia was still very strong. There was as yet no glasnost or perestroika. The Poles were in danger of being invaded. For this reason they returned to autocratic Government and elected the military Dictator General Jaruzelski. The Zomo (riot police) arrested many people, including Walesa. Solidarity was banned. Jaruzelski ruled Poland until 1989 and was probably the least bad solution to the dangerous situation in which the Poles found themselves at the start of the decade. The straw that broke the back of the Russian camel was quite possibly the Afghan War. It is unfortunately outside the scope of a book on Polish energy.

As the whole edifice tottered and collapsed in 1989 it is interesting to imagine the 39 million Poles: crafty, fiercely independent, but nevertheless not used to working. There was little to buy with their wages apart from bread and vodka. The zloty had little value. For that reason Poles carried on them huge quantities of money on the off chance that there would somewhere be a surprise delivery of a luxury, like sugar. Then a long queue would form.

It is obvious that such people would covet the material comforts of Western Europe and be keen on close ties with it. The ties could best be cemented by actual membership of the European Union. They looked on it as being elected to a Rich Man's Club. The attraction of the East to the West is obvious, but why should the West be attracted to the East?

Militarily we are still frightened of Russia. She still has tens of thousands of nuclear weapons.

A new Dictator could appear overnight just as dangerous as Stalin. Therefore we welcome a chain of countries in the buffer zone to our side. This we do via NATO however, not the EU.

Poland is now in NATO. By good luck I went to the Sheraton and heard Prime Minister Buzek's accession speech. The remarkable aspect of this was that the Warsaw Pact was dissolved in Warsaw, only a few hundred yards from the building where it was created. That happened in April 1999.

There was a chance then that Brussels, seeing that Poland was now an ally, would scale down the accession process in a sphere more economic than military. But this has not happened, for three reasons, I would suggest.

Firstly, as the Poles discover that capitalism means competition and hard work and unemployment they could be seduced by Russia to join a pan Slavic Union. Russia must now feel isolated and would certainly welcome other countries back into her fold. It would make sense to choose a subtler route than military invasion. It could be called the Russian Commonwealth.

Secondly, the East Europeans are attractive to the Westerners because they are intelligent cultured people. They surely resemble now Germany in the early 30s: a country ruined by hyper inflation but with the potential to become great again given the right catalyst. (Sadly, in Germany's case the catalyst was Hitler.)

There is a huge market waiting for the West in Eastern Europe. It is common to find GDP growing by 6% per annum.

Thirdly, the West still has a guilty conscience about its failure to support Eastern Europe before the Second World War.

Broadly speaking, Polish accession is encouraged. But on narrower issues there are problems, particularly with those countries next to Poland; Austria and Germany.

They worry about cheap Polish labour flooding the workplace and about an influx of Mafiosi across the open border with the Ukraine.

Brussels reassures these two countries on the toughness of the *Acquis*. But this in turn upsets the Poles whose national pride makes them refuse to go to Brussels on bended knee.

\* \* \*

1989 certainly marks the start of the accession process. To the ordinary Pole in the street it may have seemed like a sudden entry to a land flowing with milk and honey. But to the Government it seemed less dramatic. There were to be round table discussions between Government and Solidarity. It was expected that Jaruzelski would continue in power. Then there were to be 'free' elections to the Polish Parliament, called the Sejm, but with 65% of the seats reserved for the Polish Workers' Party.

The following happened:

Solidarity swept the board in the Sejm: that is, in the 35% of the seats where it was allowed to stand and the first Solidarity Prime Minister, Mazowiecki, was appointed. A new Upper House was created; the Senate, with 100 members. In this the Polish Workers' Party won no seats at all. Then the Polish Workers' Party was dissolved. Walesa was elected President. There followed free elections to the whole Sejm. Seats were now gained by manifold parties of all persuasions.

These changes took place over two years. When they were complete Gorbachev was still in power in Russia. The coup to restore hard line Communism had not happened.

When it did, the new Polish Democracy must have had a very anxious three days.

With the benefit of hindsight it seems that the Polish Government was slow on the uptake: it had not seen the significance of the collapse of the Berlin Wall. Neither had the Russians, the East Germans, or the Romanians.

Jaruzelski's assumptions that he would be elected President and that he would be presiding over a parliament not much changed for the next four years were simply wrong. It reminds me of the television pictures of Ceausescu addressing what he took to be an adoring mob in Bucharest. Ceausescu had been told by his surrounding sycophants that he was too good for the Romanian people. This he sincerely believed. There came a fleeting second during his address when the penny dropped. He realised that the crowd did not adore him. They hated him. He fled, and was killed two days later.

Jaruzelski was not killed, but his impressions were similarly mistaken.

As the Poles threw out the old order they surely saw a panacea in democracy. But despite their commendable spirit of independence during the Communist period they had lost all touch with it. They did not really know its meaning. They did not know how to manage different political parties, as will emerge below. Nor did they understand the law of supply and demand.

So the 90s mark the start of a turbulent period in Polish history. This was foreseen by Gorbachev when he remarked in 1980, 'for the Soviet Union, the writing is on the wall'.

In 1994 Vaclav Havel wrote:

'The modern era has been dominated by the belief, expressed in different forms, that the World, and Being as such, is a wholly knowable system governed by a finite number of universal laws that Man can group and rationally direct for his own benefit. This era, beginning in the Renaissance and developing from the enlightenment to Socialism, from positivism to scientism, from the Industrial Revolution to the Information Revolution, was characterised by rapid advances in rational cognitive thinking. This in turn gave rise to the proud belief that Man, as the pinnacle of everything that exists, was capable of objectively describing, explaining and controlling everything that exists, and of possessing the one and only truth about the World. It was an era...of belief in automatic progress brokered by the scientific method. It was an era of systems... It was an era of ideologies, doctrines, interpretations of reality, an era when the goal was to find a universal theory of the world and thus a universal key to unlock its prosperity. Communism was the perverse extreme of this trend.'

# CHAPTER 2

## Unsaddling the Socialist Cow

### 1. Solidarity: 1989-1993

As Solidarity swept into power it became apparent that they had been united only by their hatred of the Soviet system. Walesa himself had been effective in adversity, but when his Party gained office they lacked a common policy to restructure the country.

A split grew between Walesa and his ministers. These were mainly intellectuals and were tempted to laugh at an humble trade union leader whose command of the Polish language was basic. A split also developed between Solidarity and the Church over the issue of abortion.

The result was fragmentation. Between September 1989 and June 1992 there were five Prime Ministers and two general elections. Mazowiecki, the first Solidarity Prime Minister, lasted only from September 1989 to December 1990. He was succeeded by Bielecki, who found it hard to control a Sejm still dominated by the Polish Workers' Party. He lasted nine months.

There was then another general election. No seats in the Sejm were reserved for the Polish Workers' Party so this was the first genuinely free election. In it 29 parties were represented. Solidarity by now had many factions and had to contend with The Friends of Beer Party, the Union of Great Poles, the Union of Podhale and Women Against Life's Hardships. After the election the number of political parties grew, until in 1992 there were 154 of them. The Friends of Beer split into Large Beer and Small Beer. People came to say 'When two Poles meet the result is three Political Parties'.

Solidarity cobbled together a coalition. Their main opposition consisted of the old Communist Party, now reformed, together with the Peasants' Party, known as the Watermelon Party as it was green on the outside but red within.

Walesa installed Jan Olszewski as new Prime Minister. He lasted only six months, until June 1992. There was then a feud between President and Prime Minister over de-Communisation.

Pawlak of the Peasants' Party was next chosen by Walesa, but he was unable to form a workable coalition.

There were frequent allegations that Ministers had in the past been working for the Russians.

Walesa himself was accused of doing so. He was accused of being a confidential agent of the Secret Police in the 70s, using the alias 'Bolek'. Many Poles were removed from office through a process called 'lustration', which was an investigation into their past to reveal connections they may have had with the Russians.

After the Pawlak failure Walesa appointed Hanna Suchocka as Prime Minister. She lasted a year. In June 1993 the Government lost a vote of no confidence and that was the end of Solidarity's first period in power.

This first phase of freedom showed the Poles that democracy had many pitfalls and they did not produce either President or Prime Minister strong enough to overcome them. There was no Margaret Thatcher.

Leszek Balcerowicz came closest to providing the tough measures needed to transform Poland from command to demand economy. He was Finance Minister and is known for his 'Shock Therapy'. He himself preferred to call it 'Spring Therapy' as the word 'shock' has negative connotations. But he nevertheless regarded it as essential to, 'jump into the water blindfold without first testing the depth or the length of the drop.'

Balcerowicz had taught at Sussex University and was advised by the American economist Jeffrey Sachs. Sachs had had success reforming the hyper inflationary economies of South America. Balcerowicz's measures caused widespread unemployment but ten years on they are seen as the only means that could possibly have made the Polish economy viable.

As I have said above it was not really possible to cost anything in Poland before 1989.

When Balcerowicz attempted to do so he found, not surprisingly, that the country was desperately poor. His measures were aimed at attracting foreign investment.

He was looking for the financing of major projects, a speed up of privatisation, a transfer of modern technology, an increase in product differentiation and most important of all, a reduction in the balance of payments deficit.

The route to these goals was beset by pain and dissent. For instance, the price of coal rose by 600% in January 1990. Even so the coal industry lost 360 million dollars in 1990 and a billion dollars in 1991.

In 1992, the Government raised the price of electricity, hot water and energy products by 100%. These were desperate measures indeed, but Balcerowicz faced a desperate situation.

For instance there was in 1991 a budget deficit of 30 trillion zlotys. 23 trillion of this was due to unpaid tax by State firms.

In *Anatomy of the New Poland* Frances Millard (Reader in East European Politics, Portsmouth University) writes, 'The changes in 1989 marked the beginning of the transformation of elements of the nomenklatura from a group merely controlling the means of production to actually owning them, which was potentially more lucrative.'

1989 also marked the start of the Polish Mafiosi and a general feeling that the Balcerowicz plan was simply a part of a Western conspiracy to bankrupt their country. As for the ordinary Polish workers, they went on strike. 'Only' 87 times in the first half of 1990, but 360 in the second half.

The actual extent of the Polish economic crisis of the early 90s can best be demonstrated by the declining value of the zloty. In 1995, with the crisis over, the Poles re-valued it. One new zloty equalled 10,000 old zlotys. (There were around 6.5 new zlotys to the pound in 2000.)

Balcerowicz's philosophy is that change must be sudden, as if it is gradual it is modified, weakened, and may not happen at all. His achievements included a trade surplus with Russia of 2.5 billion roubles, and of 1.4 billion with the other former socialist countries.

He achieved some price reductions between 1990 and 1993:
  Milk: from 5,043 pln to 820 (pln is the abbreviation of zloty).
  Bread: 1,017 to 597.
  Cheese: 201 to 144 per kg.
  Theatre tickets: 454 to 159.

His shock therapy was supported from the start by the International Monetary Fund and the World Bank.

In April 1991 the Paris Club of the Organisation of Economic Co-operation and Development (OECD) Governments agreed to write off approximately half of Poland's international debt. This was followed by a similar deal with the private London Club Banks. This created a breathing space until the early twenty-first century, when repayment obligations will increase sharply.

Drastic measures were needed to meet a drastic change. The difficulty of change from socialist to capitalist system was predictable, but that corruption at the top should make the change even harder came as a nasty surprise.

Olszewski, Prime Minister in 1992, put it well when he said, 'The invisible hand of the market has often turned out to be the hand of the swindler, garnering public funds from the State Treasury'.

The difficulty is epitomised in the Olszewski Government's plan to restructure the coal industry, approved by the Council of Ministers in May 1992. If implemented it would have permanently closed eleven unprofitable mines in 1993 and laid off some 40,000 workers. These moves would accelerate the modernisation and development of profitable mines. These mines would then be commercialised and integrated into seven syndicates strong enough to handle market competition.

The plan raised questions. The cost of closing one mine was reckoned to be between US$75-100 million. No funds had been set aside for this in the budget. It was unlikely that funds would be voted in future budgets, even assuming that these closures would be politically feasible. Furthermore, the creation of bodies to supervise the seven mining syndicates could lead to the re-creation of the middle level Communist bureaucracy that was the bane of economic reform during the 1980s.

The mining syndicates' real functions would probably be:

1. Using revenues from profitable mines to keep unprofitable mines afloat.

2. Promoting cartel like behaviour amongst coal sellers.

3. Bargaining with central authorities for increased subsidies and protection from market forces.

If so, this would have the opposite effect of that intended.

But as said above, Olszewski fell, Suchocka fell, and the Solidarity coalition itself was to fall in the general election of 1993.

## 2. The Return of the Communists: 1993 to 1997

The 1993 election was to be more like those in the longer established democracies of the West. New legislation decreed that no delegate could be elected unless his party commanded 5% of the national vote. This relegated oddballs like the Small Beer Party into the same area as that occupied by the late Screaming Lord Sutch in the United Kingdom.

The new Government ushered in a period of stability. They were not at all like the old communists ruling before 1989. They saw themselves as practical people. 'Solidarity plans new super highways. We mend the roads.' That was their philosophy.

However the neo-Communists themselves could only obtain a majority in the Sejm by allying with the Peasants' Party. These Communists, or SLD, won 171 seats and the Peasants, or PSL, won 131. That amounted to 66% of the seats in the Sejm.

Once back in Government the two parties found themselves increasingly at odds. The SLD needed to cut industrial and agricultural subsidies to improve the climate for foreign investment in order to achieve its growth and anti inflation targets. The PSL, in contrast, remained loyal to its small farmer base, with its continued attachment to protectionism and subsidised credit, and misgivings over privatisation.

The first Prime Minister was Pawlak, from the Peasants' Party, whom Walesa had asked to form a Government a year earlier, without success.

He was suspicious of the West, saying, 'Our contemporary pro Europeanism is turning into an ideology of servility towards the wealthy capitalist world'.

Whilst Pawlak was against privatisation, he did favour 'rationalisation of company management'. It was he who turned 3,500 companies that were formerly mere arms of Government into joint stock companies wholly owned by the Treasury. For the first time such companies found out if they were profitable.

By June of 1994 Balcerowicz's shock therapy was also yielding dividends.

17,577 companies with foreign capital had invested in Poland by:

1. Privatisation of the state sector.
2. Greenfield developments.
3. Co-operation with Poland as a private partner.

There was US$4bn of foreign money in Poland, from these countries, in order of magnitude:

USA
Italy
Germany
France
UK
Holland

Pawlak was followed by Oleksy in February 1995. He fell foul of a new Lustration Law. This obliged every minister to sign a declaration that he had never worked for the Soviet Union. Oleksy was unable to sign. He was succeeded by Cimoszewicz in January 1996.

But the more important election was the Presidential one of 1995. Lech Walesa, hero of the Gdansk shipyards and Solidarity, was defeated by the neo-Communist Kwasniewski. Thus the SLD had both Prime Minister and President.

The President of Poland has a veto, which can only be overturned by a two-thirds majority in the Sejm. The SLD and PSL had 66% of the seats. They actually needed 66.66% to overturn him. This was however not a serious issue as the President belonged to the majority party.

It was to become more serious after the general election of 1997 and the return of a new Solidarity coalition. Presidents are elected for five-year terms. The next election was in 2000. Kwasniewski was elected for a second term.

In July of 1997 Poland had appalling floods. The Vistula burst its banks. The Oder and Neisse turned into raging torrents and destroyed thousands of peasant dwellings. Prime Minister Cimoszewicz was criticised for not building better flood defences and then not helping the peasants to repair and rebuild. His reply, 'people should have been insured', was the arrogant remark that helped his party to lose the 1997 general election. The election was due in any event since the Sejm had reached the end of its four-year statutory period allowed under the new constitution.

## 3. The Return of Solidarity

The SLD suffered a massive defeat in 1997. It was not that their own vote collapsed so much as that the Peasants' Party's vote was all but annihilated. SLD seats fell from 171 to 164 and the Peasants' from 131 to 27.

The major party now became Solidarity Electoral Action, known as AWS with 201 seats. This was a loose confederation of Solidarity factions. Krzazklewski is the key figure. He took over the leadership of Solidarity from Lech Walesa. He forged a coalition with the centre right wing Freedom Union Party, known as UW, and headed by Leszek Balcerowicz. With the 60 UW seats the new coalition had an overall majority in the Sejm.

Krzazklewski decided against being Prime Minister himself. He appointed Jerzy Buzek, regarded by some as Krzazklewski's placeman. Be that as it may, he has stayed in office for three and a half years and is thus the longest serving Polish Prime Minister since independence.

What of AWS itself? It is certainly an amalgamation of many different solidarity factions.

Cynics define it as the National, Christian, Democratic, Conservative, Liberal, Agrarian, Socialist Party. It is not strictly a party but a bloc of many factions ranging from the liberal SLK to the authoritarian Catholic Radio Maria which has worrying anti-Semitic tendencies.

The SLD is also a bloc rather than a party, but it has an identity of sorts. AWS was born simply to capture power. Its founding declaration states its goal as, 'the founding of a broad electoral bloc which will have a chance of winning the next election.'

A loose confederation like AWS must be doomed. As it entered the new millennium, more and more factions started to vote against Government in general and Buzek in particular.

Balcerowicz and his UW Party eventually told AWS that if it was impossible for them to find a prime minister whom all factions could support then UW would leave the coalition. This has now happened and AWS are a minority government with no teeth. It is reckoned that they will cling on to power until January 2001 when there will be a general election. SLD is likely to win and Balcerowicz's UW Party could make itself a bedfellow with SLD. The President, Kwasniewski, was re-elected in October 2000. Since he is SLD a period of less political party infighting is desirable and even possible.

From an early stage however, all party blocs have been cursed by a dangerous utopian streak. For instance, the Peasants' Party fell because it was based on the false assumption that it is possible to have private property without a private owner. Privatisation legislation actually slows down the process. Businesses are confronted with more than 220 laws passed over the previous 60 years and amended approximately 500 times. Not surprisingly, of the fifty companies intended for privatisation in 1998 only eighteen succeeded. Beneath the many yards of bureaucratic red tape lies the true opponent of change: that is, organised labour. The Unions are opposed to privatisation but not affiliated to one political grouping. For instance, the 18 mining unions are split between SLD and AWS.

Employee self-management councils can choose both a company's management and how to distribute its profits. They can and do decide that all profits should be soaked up in wage increases. AWS's current inability to restructure the mining sector is responsible for a debt of 15 billion zlotys in that sector alone. Polish economic development as a whole must suffer until trade union domination over the economy is removed. Neither of the loose groupings of parties under AWS or SLD seems to have the muscle to do this.

But it is not all bad news. Economic growth in Poland has exceeded 7% annually. Poland has attracted foreign direct investment (FDI) at the staggering rate of a million dollars an hour. In the first six years of transition the private sector came to represent 63% of gross domestic product (GDP). The actual total of FDI up to the end of 1998 is US$30 billion. This has led the President of Poland's National Bank to predict that Poland will be joining the Single European Currency only one year after her target accession date of January 1 2003.

In conclusion, the new Poland has conflicting features that should result in chaos but actually result in a considerable measure of success:

A plethora of political parties that are not even parties; merely groupings. Oceans of red tape. Militant Trade Unions. Result? The most successful of the new Eastern European economies.

Dr Frances Millard attributes four unique features to Poland:
1. A thriving religion.
2. An assertive working class.
3. A land owning peasantry.
4. A vigorous intelligentsia.

As to the key figure since 1989, I would suggest Leszek Balcerowicz. He has refuted Pushkin's famous dictum that Polish history has been and ought to be a disaster.

# CHAPTER 3

## Black Gold: Poland's Fuel

Polish Coal Mines

Brown Coal

Black Coal, Silesia and Lublin

No country in Europe is more dependent on coal than Poland.

This was Poland's energy balance 1996 (million tonnes of oil equivalent):

|           | Oil  | Gas  | Coal | Electricity | Other | Total |
|-----------|------|------|------|-------------|-------|-------|
| Production| 0.3  | 4    | 87.1 | 0.9         | 4.7   | 97    |
| Imports   | 17.5 | 6.1  | 1.4  | 1           | 0     | 26    |
| Exports   | 0.9  | 0    | 16.5 | 1.6         | 0     | 19    |
| **Total** | **16.9** | **10.1** | **72** | **0.3** | **4.7** | **104** |

(Economist Intelligence Unit, 1997)

Coal powered Poland and, as explained earlier, the Communists saw the provision of light, heat and power as a social duty. There was no question of making it profitable. Cost factors were of little relevance in powering factories, with the result that energy use in all sectors was high relative to Western countries. This difference increased after 1974 because Poland was not subject to the energy conservation measures adopted by the West in response to high oil prices.

Mining had previously been firmly protected from any logic of the market and its finances were totally incomprehensible. There was a baffling heritage of past subsidy with seemingly illogical variations between individual mines, which made it very hard to predict how finances, and hence wages, would move if steps were taken towards a market economy.

Energy production from coal was dirty. There was no good reason to clean it up. Thus plant and methods became frozen in time, so much so that when they were exposed to the harsh light of the market place, Balcerowicz pronounced that the cheapest and cleanest option was to scrap the lot and build combined cycle turbines powered by Russian gas.

'Shut every mine. Sack half a million miners. Do not try to clean up the power stations. Knock them down and rebuild from scratch.'

Now, in the new millennium, only 11 of the 66 mines have been closed. Only 10 of the 33 power stations have been fitted with flue gas desulphurisation equipment and low Nox burners. None have been pulled down. A quarter of them are more than 40 years old. None of them are gas fired.

There are indeed plans to increase the amount of gas burn as thereby Poland will more easily comply with the Kyoto maxima, but these are only plans. Gas needs a separate section in this book, as indeed do other types of fuel. First it is important to look at Poland's coal culture, as it is similar to other coal cultures throughout the world.

Deep mined coal alone generates pollution that is subsidised by the Government, as it is in England, and Germany.

Coal-miners are a uniquely powerful lobby. They brought down the Heath Government in 1974. It is well known that the United Kingdom was cursed by a series of miners' strikes after the Second World War. In Poland in 1989, the miners scored a great victory. The Solidarity Party which they had supported in 1980 finally came to power. In 1991 their champion Lech Walesa became President. But then they went on strike.

This surprising bit of timing can be explained in part by a fall in the real value of their wages.

The early 90s were a period of great turmoil and inflation. Miners were traditionally paid well; that is, around double the national average industrial wage. In 1991 this sank to 58% above average. That was sufficient to cause the strike.

Miners are unlike other workers. They are a tightly knit community. They most likely all live in the same village. They have great pride in their work. The work is dangerous, though it is not highly skilled. Value added to each tonne of coal from mineface to pithead is not great.

They are superstitious and religious. Their patron saint is Saint Barbara.

Actually, they much resemble a regiment. They even have their own brass bands. They have messes. There is heavy drinking. Loyalty to the unit is absolute. It is possible to look upon miners as a State within a State. They will do anything for their unit, but feel no great loyalty to central Government.

When a tightly knit group like this decides to withhold its labour it is targeting an amorphous mass simply known as 'The Public'. The public is not tightly knit. They find it hard to organise any opposition. Therefore their representatives, the Government, find that the easiest solution is to penalise the public by raising the price of coal. They do this either indirectly, by subsidy, or directly by charging customers more.

When the Polish miners struck in 1991, the price of coal had already risen the year before by 600%. That was the extent of the culture shock of the change to democracy: a six-fold price increase, with a miners' strike on top of it.

The whole Mickey Mouse nature of coal mining maths was exposed by the ending of the command economy. In the year of the strike the coal industry lost a billion dollars. The next year 60 of the 66 mines were in the red. In 1998 the industry lost US$8 billion.

The most articulate anti coal-lobby are the managers of large industrial plants. It is they who can see the advantage in both cost and cleanliness in a switch to gas. Indeed forward plans from the Government do show Poland 50% reliant on gas by 2008. A cynic might say that 2008 is a comfortable distance away.

With 165,000 miners and another half million jobs dependent on the mines it is quite unrealistic to expect a democratically elected Government to embark on a United Kingdom type 'Dash for Gas'. That would merely guarantee that they lost the next election.

This problem was exemplified by a meeting between the Leader of the Silesian Parliament, Jan Olbrycht, and John McDowall CBE, the head of British Steel (now the Anglo Dutch 'Corus') which I arranged at Westminster in November 1999. Corus is investing in the colossal Katowice steel works built by Gierek in the 1970s.

McDowall simply told Olbrycht that British Steel's workforce had been reduced from 80,000 to 12,000 and that they were now making more steel of higher quality. If Olbrycht could promise a similar reduction Corus would invest US$50 million in Huta Katowice. Olbrycht looked uncomfortable and said, 'But I want to be re-elected'.

Incidentally, Corus has invested in a steelworks in Alabama which employs 400 people and produces as much steel as Huta

Katowice which employs 15,000 people. This example concerns steel, not coal: but that the same principle applies to coal is evident in the fact that the British miner produces seven times as much coal as his Polish counterpart.

Polish mines are overmanned, yet sacking three quarters of the work force is a clear vote loser.

Strangely, the only period during which the Poles could have made such a reduction, together with a switch to gas, was the Communist one. That that never happened was firstly because the Russians felt pollution unimportant, and secondly because their precious natural gas could earn hard currency if exported to the then ECC. Also, most importantly, coal is Poland's only fuel.

It is unfair to compare the Poles with economies such as our own when we can if we prefer use our own gas, our own oil, even our own nuclear power. Coal is the only fuel that is truly Polish and to expect Poles to abandon it in favour of a foreign source is arrogant and unrealistic.

Russian gas is a non-starter from Poland's point of view. Therefore the Polish Government is taking the only realistic course. This is to clean up emissions from both mines and power stations and to reduce the number of miners.

This is no easy task. Within the Government there is a powerful miners' lobby.

In particular Ministers in the Department of Energy are usually former miners, irrespective of party affiliation, as the following list shows:

1992 Andrjes Lipko SLD
1993/4 Morawski UW
1995/7 Scierski PSL
Markowski SLD
Steinhoff AWS
1998-9 Jan Szlazak AWS

I met Szlazak in the spring of 1999 and when I asked him about the price of coal he replied that it was, simply, the market price. There was no subsidy.

In the summer of 2000 I met Lucjan Noras, the President of Poland's domestic coal marketing agency Weglozbyt. He told me that Poland was in a transitional period and that coal prices could not be determined until that period was over. However he said that Polish coal is actually cheaper than Australian coal provided ancillary miners' benefits such as housing and health are excluded.

On the face of it this seems an absurd statement, for deep mined coal cannot compete with open cast. However the cost of transporting foreign coal on Poland's railways is very high. There are no canals to provide an alternative to rail and the road system is hugely congested. So Mr Noras's statement is probably right if coal must be carried three hundred miles to the main cluster of power stations in Silesia.

Mr Noras told me that Australian coal would be cheaper if the power station was on the Baltic coast, though it would be extremely expensive to build unloading facilities at Gdansk or Szczecin. At the moment coal is only loaded at these ports, for export. It would seem a simple matter to make the ship to shore conveyor belts reversible. Noras admitted that Polish deep coal-mines run at a loss and continued, more surprisingly, that, 'since the Government will not compensate them, tax evasion is inevitable. Prices,' he states, 'are freely negotiated between mines and power stations.'

The Brussels view differs from those of both Szlazak and Noras. The part of the Commission specialising in energy, DG TREN wrote in their paper 'Synergy in Poland' that, 'Price fixing in Poland is widespread and needs to be addressed if the conditions of the European Coal and Steel Community are to be complied with'.

The National Grid, or PSE, is really an arm of Government and here too miners rule the roost, for instance; Popczyk of UW and Zmijewski of AWS are both former miners.

The Department of the Environment, in contrast, strongly supports a reduction in the work force and the clean up of emissions. Traditionally this department is rather weak. What is clear is that the departments are not 'singing from the same hymn sheet'. President Kwasniewski and Prime Minister Buzek therefore have their work cut out in carrying through any mutually agreed policy.

They are dealing with a creature now known as Homo Sovieticus: someone who has been a Communist for most of his life and set in his ways. Once part of a privileged elite, or nomenklatura, he must now fight his own corner. Even worse, he might be tempted by corruption.

Beyond a peradventure, accusations of dishonest behaviour are more widespread in Poland than in the West.

* * *

Out of this welter of conflicting ideals and moralities it is now necessary to assess what successive Polish Governments have actually done about coal.

The Olszewski plan of 1992 to group mines into seven syndicates was intended to close down the unprofitable mines, to reduce production, and to make the whole hard coal industry profitable. Each group was to become a joint stock company wholly owned by the Treasury.

When it was eventually implemented it had the feared effect of enabling good mines to subsidise bad mines within the same group. The syndicates became a cartel able to fix the price of coal. There was still over-production with 4.3 million tonnes stockpiled at the power stations and a further 7.2 million tonnes at the pitheads in 1998.

The coal industry is concentrated in Upper Silesia, Lower Silesia, and Lublin in the South East. Upper Silesia is easily the biggest producer. Five out of fifty-nine pits were closed there. Lower Silesia had small and expensive pits. Six of these were closed. Indeed coal mining in Lower Silesia is all but finished.

To offset these reductions there was an increase in production from the Lublin field, where the coal is more accessible, so much so that each miner produces 1,500 tonnes of coal per year, compared to an average 600 tonnes. This mine, at Bogdanka, is so profitable that it will be privatised, and I am informed by the Head of the Hard Coal Restructuring Agency Zygmunt Smolec that there are plenty of Western companies interested in it.

This is the situation in detail, in 1996. Mines are in light type, groupings in bold type:

**Bytomska Group, 13,041,130 tonnes** made up as follows:

| | |
|---|---|
| Andaluzja | 1,799,700 |
| Julian | 1,986,300 |
| Rozbark | 1,564,750 |
| Centrum Szombierki | 2,315,200 |
| Powstancow Slaskich | 1,506,820 |
| Bobrek | 1,292,850 |
| Miechowice | 1,152,950 |
| Jowisz | 746,610 (to be closed) |
| Grodziec | 675,950 (to be closed) |

**Rudska Group, 14,330,200 tonnes** made up as follows:

| | |
|---|---|
| Halemba | 4,527,200 |
| Polska Wirek | 1,883,300 |
| Pokoi | 2,633,200 |
| Siemianowice | 0 (to be closed) |
| Zaklad Gorniczy Rosalia | 1,171,000 |
| Zabrze-Bielsowice | 4,115,500 |

**Gliwicka Group, 18,191,623 tonnes** made up as follows:

| | |
|---|---|
| Bolesalw Smialy | 2,350,355 |
| Debiensko | 1,816,360 |
| Gliwice | 1,110,561 |
| Knurow | 3,046,344 |
| Makoszowy | 3,249,040 |
| Sosnica | 3,584,300 |
| Szczyglowice | 3,034,663 |

**Katowicka Group, 23,902,404 tonnes** made up as follows:

| | |
|---|---|
| Katowice Kleofas | 3,210,000 |

| | |
|---|---|
| Kazimierz Juliusz | 1,011,250 (to be closed) |
| Murcki | 2,649,900 |
| Myslowice | 2,000,050 |
| Niwka Modrzejow | 1,396,164 (to be closed) |
| Wesola | 4,039,200 |
| Wieczorek1 | 898,500 |
| Wujek | 2,058,950 |
| Staszic | 3,721,940 |
| Slask | 1,916,540 |

**Nadwislanska Group, 23,703,468 tonnes** made up as follows:

| | |
|---|---|
| Brzeszcze | 2,272,400 |
| Czeczott | 3,144,100 |
| Janina | 2,475,240 |
| Jaworzno | 2,129,059 |
| Piast | 5,200,000 |
| Siersza | 1,149,694 |
| Silesia | 1,135,550 |
| Ziemowit | 5,749,425 |

**Rybnicka Group, 15,782,523 tonnes** made up as follows:

| | |
|---|---|
| Rydultowy | 2,417,200 |
| Anna | 1,894,552 |
| Marcel | 3,754,021 |
| Chwalowice | 3,252,750 |
| Jankowice | 4,464,000 |

**Jastrzebska Group, 16,741,751 tonnes** made up as follows:

| | |
|---|---|
| Borynia | 2,522,300 |
| Jas-Mos | 4,127,000 |
| Krupinski | 2,460,051 |
| Morcinek | 1,281,150 |
| Pniowek | 3,402,000 |
| Zofiowka | 2,949,250 |

INDEPENDENT MINES:

**10,533,295 tonnes,** made up as follows:

| | |
|---|---|
| Bogdanka | 3,602,500 |
| Bodryk | 1,862,365 |
| Jan Kanty | 1,029,100 |
| Porabka Klimontow | 760,700 |
| Grodziec | 188,500 |
| Kazimierz Julius | 191,833 |
| Niwka Modrzejow | 237,312 |
| Jowisz | 250,000 |
| Siemianowice | 0 (to be closed) |
| Saturn | 0 (to be closed) |
| Sosnowiec | 658,000 |
| Paryz | 0 (to be closed) |
| ZWP Antracytu | 233,925 |
| ZWSM Jadwiga | 525,107 |
| Zory | 0 (to be closed) |
| Pstrowski | 0 (to be closed) |
| Walbrzyskie | 119,866 (to be closed) |
| Nowa Ruda | 458,752 |

Total tonnes mined for the year: 136,226,394.

(Statistics from the Hard Coal Restructuring Agency, Katowice.)

*The Economist* (3rd quarter 1998) confirms that production steadied to around 135 to 137 million tonnes between 1995 and 1997.

Figures for earlier years are:

1989: 192 million tonnes

1990: 148 million

1994/5: 130 million.

Thus the 1996 figures show a huge decrease from the late eighties, but strangely, an increase of 6 million tonnes above the previous two years.

What is more, Polish internal demand sank from 118 million to 110 million tonnes between 1990 and 1996. So the figure of 136,226,394 tonnes quoted for 1996 leaves a balance of some 26 million tonnes for stockpiling or for export, of which more later.

The basic problem is that current volumes of output cannot be sold.

The hard coal industry is loss-making and heavily in debt.

The 11 closures listed above are insignificant and it is fair to say that the industry has so far proved immune to basic restructuring.

The number of miners has decreased much more than the tonnage mined, thus:

1988 - 489,000 miners.

1995 - 375,300 miners.

1996 - 293,000 miners.

1998 - 235,000 miners.

Thus if tonnage were related to manpower it would have more than halved. It would be a mere 96 million tonnes which is actually less than Poland needs herself. But the miners who leave do so from the least productive mines.

The present Government has brought down the number of miners even more. At the end of 1998 there were just over 207,000. In 2000 165,000. The target is 125,000 in 2002.

The miners are leaving in numbers greater than expected by the Government. The forecast figure was 11,000 for 1998. The actual figure was 32,000. Incentives to leave are high. There is an offer of 'Mining Leave' which is 70% of the last month's salary for two years. Most miners prefer a lump sum payment equal to £8,000, and actually worth three times that as the cost of living in Poland is only one third of the UK's.

As mentioned above, the mining tradition in Poland is only 50 years old, unlike the UK's 200 years. Many Poles moved to Silesia from their small farms in other parts of Poland when Stalin and Gomulka made it attractive for them to do so in the 50s and 60s. Now many find it equally attractive to return to their farms with a fat cheque in their pocket.

Unfortunately the Government had not budgeted for so many leavers and so was unable to pay the promised lump sum without borrowing. Poland has therefore turned to both the World Bank and the EBRD (European Bank for Reconstruction and Development) for aid. The World Bank is lending US$1 billion. US$300 million of this covered half the restructuring costs for just one year: 1998.

The European Union has already approved a grant of 20 million euros for redundancy payments.

The redundancy payments must make economic sense. The day cannot be far off when there is a substantial decrease in hard coal production.

But it is worth bearing in mind that Polish electricity consumption per capita is well below that of the EU, at 3.4 megawatt hours (Mwh) compared to 5.8 Mwh. As the Polish standard of living rises so will electrical consumption. It would clearly be wrong to increase coal production once more to meet this increase. The preferred fuel should surely be gas, or possibly nuclear.

\* \* \*

In the spring of 1999 I met Dr Jerzy Markowski, who is a Senator and was Minister for Mines in the last SLD Government. He is a former miner himself. He agreed with my figures above: that coal production is still running 30% in excess of demand. However he did not approve of redundancies. 40,000 redundant miners would cost Poland more than subsidising the export of coal they would have produced if they were still working.

Markowski claimed that Poland's coal production had halved in the last ten years. This does not accord with my figures.

Markowski is very pro coal. He also saw German mines closing as a result of environmental pressure and suggested that German coal should be replaced by Polish coal. Poland, at the very centre of Europe, is uniquely well placed to export coal to all neighbouring countries, and he felt that this would be viable within an 800km radius of Silesia.

He scotched my comment that this would mean a massive subsidy by blaming the railways, with reason, as it costs more to transport a tonne of coal from Silesia to Gdansk than it does to mine it.

I cannot accept that the West would import more Polish coal, but it might import Polish electricity. Kyoto targets require Western Europe to reduce emissions but Eastern Europe, including Poland, can increase them. The Poles could build more power stations to supply Germany and close the Ruhr mines, to the chagrin of German power station moguls perhaps, but to the delight of the environmentalists.

Markowski claimed that under the SLD the efficiency of the mines increased by 20%, but under AWS indebtedness had increased by 200%. The mining industry debt now equals two years of production. Mr Markowski was in Opposition when I met him.

\* \* \*

Not surprisingly, the AWS Government take a very different view of coal from Mr Markowski and the SLD. AWS has produced a new document 'Reform of the hard coal mining industry, 1998-2002', which would be the more convincing if so many earlier reforms had not fallen by the wayside.

It starts by stating that 'The economical and financial state of the coal industry dramatically deteriorated in the last two years' (of SLD government!). It makes the sound point that though 96/97 figures were indeed a decrease on 1988 they were way above SLD's forecasts. These were for 127 million tonnes mined in '96 and 125 million in '97. Thus the actual '96 figure was 9 million tonnes over forecast, at 136 million.

One would hope to find realistic future policies in such a document, which is of 74 pages. On page 12 appears a prognosis of future production, some of which has already been proved wrong.

AWS reduced targets per annum: millions of tonnes of hard coal:

1998: 116
1999: 116.5
2000: 114
2001: 112
2002: 110

On page 16 we get: 'The coal companies will not be generating losses on operational activities as of the year 2000.'

On page 18: 'Therefore it is necessary to create, through legal regulations, the basis enabling the annulment of interests and a considerable part of the main liabilities due to the main creditors.'

On page 18, even more depressingly, it becomes apparent that most of the 11 mines marked as 'to be closed' in my master list of 1996, were still 'preparing for closure' in 1998.

However, a substantial allocation of nearly one billion zlotys is allocated for restructuring, including 211 million for liquidation. The means of reducing the workforce to 125 thousand seems to be working and on schedule. 'The total cost for all the intended results will be 4.3 billion zlotys.'

It is easy to be sceptical about such a document. It is certainly optimistic. However, it was accepted by resolution of the Government on 30 June 1998 and it actually became law on 14 Jan 1999.

It is therefore the best tool that the Poles have to reform the hard coal industry.

* * *

The World Bank reckons Polish coal mining losses over recent years as follows:

2.2 billion zlotys in 1996

3.3 billion zlotys in 1997

4.0 billion zlotys in 1998.

The syndicates making the biggest losses, with the worst first, are:

Nadwislanka
Jastrzebska
Katowicki
Gliwicka
Rudzka Spolka.

It is difficult to get the true picture with such contradictory versions of the state of the mines.

For instance:

'The Government remains confident that the industry can move into profit next year and begin repaying debts in 2000' (Polish Department of Energy).

And, from Aleksandra Prus of the US Foreign and Commercial Service:

'The amount of coal extracted should fall from the current 137 million tonnes to 112 million tonnes with the ultimate goal of 80 million tonnes'.

The American accountants Price Waterhouse believe that the target of 80 million tonnes should be achieved immediately and the number of mines reduced to 35 if the industry is to be genuinely profitable.

Within the system there are some odd mines. Siersza, for instance, is now a co-operative, selling direct to the public with the slogan 'Siersza coal is the cheapest coal'. It is also the highest in sulphur.

The whole Bytom Group is now so indebted that the Government is considering confiscating the Mines' Presidents' assets: their houses, weekend cottages, cars, even their handkerchiefs. One of the Presidents has remarked that a handkerchief will not be much good with the following unpaid in 1999 alone:

1,800 million zlotys of VAT

6,200 million zlotys of National Insurance

5,100 million zlotys of voivodship conservation funds

3,100 million zlotys for supplies and services.

That is a total of 21 billion zlotys, or 5 billion US dollars.

A former Mining President said:

'The financial state of our country has always been so hopeless that we have had only two possibilities: either not to pay the State or not to pay the workers. The latter course would lead to riots.'

Actually the State itself has made tax evasion easier. In the previous fiscal act VAT avoidance was a serious crime, but in the new 1999 act it has been demoted to a minor offence. This milder fiscal act is actually being used against the director of the Bytom Mine, Tomasz Pawelczak.

Bytom is by no means the worst group. It is being used as a guinea pig for the others.

\* \* \*

Just as it is possible that the Government paints a picture that is too rosy, it is also possible that the picture painted at Bytom is too bleak.

For an impartial view that may have matters in the right balance I returned to the Hard Coal Restructuring Agency and Zygmunt Smolec.

He told me that Poland is now receiving funds for retraining from the EU. The key point is that Poland will receive one billion euros in 2000, compared to 400 million in 1999. I visited

Brussels two weeks later and they confirmed those figures. Smolec made the good point that mine closures were not as significant as reduction in working faces, and that neither were as significant as a reduction in total production. This is on course. In 1997 Poland produced 135 million tonnes and its target for 1999 was 116 million. It actually produced a mere 109 million. This was due to the spread of gas and a lower than predicted growth in GDP. He told me also that even with thousands of miners leaving, the unemployment rate in Silesia is quite good: 10% compared to the national average of 13.6%.

Regarding the massive debts of the mines, Smolec made the point that the mines were in profit last year, for the first time ever, provided the debts are excluded. This is a big proviso, but before 1999 the mines still lost money using the same criteria. Smolec believes that by 2003, which is the accession year to the EU, the mines will have managed to pay back all outstanding VAT and ZUS (National Insurance). He believes that the Ministry of the Economy would write off the remainder of the debt.

Smolec felt 'considerably more optimistic than two years ago' when I first met him.

The timing of that remark was unfortunate, for outside the council building there was a mass of protesting miners during our meeting. They were after a 30% pay rise, thereby breaking the Government's maximum of 7%, and an extra holiday on St Barbara's day. Smolec told me that they belonged to 'August 18': the most extreme of the 17 Miners Unions. They were nothing to worry about.

With such conflicting reports there does however seem quite a lot for the EU to worry about with regard to the Polish hard coal industry.

* * *

The coal industry's main customers are the power stations. This is such a big subject that it needs its own chapter. I will first look at coal's other uses, then mention other fuels in Poland, before I return to the principal use: the generation of electricity.

# CHAPTER 4

## Coal Exports

Poland mines more coal than she needs. Around 11 million tonnes of it are stockpiled at pithead and power station. Around 20 million tonnes are exported. Traditionally, this has been Poland's main earner of foreign exchange. It is not clear whether this was profitable for Poland before 1989. After that however, with the free market economy and the rise in miners' wages, Poland came to realise that she could not compete with the principal coal exporters such as Australia, South Africa, and Colombia, unless she subsidised her exports.

Thus at my meeting with Jan Szlazak, Minister for Mines in 1999, I also asked him about the amount of subsidy for exported coal. He replied, 'Naturally we must subsidise. We must bring it down to the world price.'

It is indeed the case that the price of Polish exported coal is around half the price of domestic coal. The Poles lose less money by exporting at half price than by stockpiling for no price. But this does cause difficulties of accession to the EU, as it is illegal to subsidise exports. It also causes a certain amount of grief in those Western European countries who still have their own deep mined coal industries.

The principal Polish coal exporter is the company Weglokoks and I list below the table of exports.

# Polish coal exports: steam coal 1996 - 1998 (000 tonnes)

|  | 1996 | 1997 | 1998 |
|---|---|---|---|
| Austria | 666.1 | 690.3 | 837.9 |
| Belgium | 313.5 | 401.8 | 323.9 |
| Belarus | 1.5 | 1.1 | 0.0 |
| Croatia | 0.0 | 0.0 | 61.0 |
| Czech Republic | 935.1 | 738.3 | 695.4 |
| Denmark | 2,431.4 | 3,281.1 | 2,384.5 |
| Finland | 3,009.2 | 2,992.8 | 1,440.4 |
| France | 624.0 | 499.5 | 1,747.0 |
| Germany | 1,067.2 | 951.4 | 3,942.2 |
| Hungary | 158.9 | 40.1 | 0.9 |
| Ireland | 263.1 | 330.1 | 240.7 |
| Israel | 0.0 | 0.0 | 62.3 |
| Italy | 253.9 | 130.5 | 127.2 |
| Latvia | 47.8 | 0.0 | 0.5 |
| Lithuania | 10.2 | 8.1 | 15.5 |
| Morocco | 0.0 | 59.9 | 124.9 |
| Moldova | 0.0 | 6.6 | 0.0 |
| Netherlands | 580.3 | 677.8 | 991.5 |
| Norway | 124.3 | 77.0 | 142.9 |
| Portugal | 2.3 | 0.0 | 0.0 |
| Russia | 75.7 | 9.9 | 1.4 |
| Serbia | 0.7 | 0.2 | 0.0 |
| Slovak Republic | 79.8 | 151.2 | 239.3 |
| Slovenia | 6.5 | 3.8 | 7.5 |
| Spain | 0.0 | 0.0 | 2.3 |
| Sweden | 514.1 | 354.1 | 464.7 |
| Ukraine | 32.4 | 0.0 | 0.0 |
| UK | 725.9 | 633.9 | 1,127.0 |
| Yugoslavia | 0.0 | 0.0 | 0.2 |
| **Total** | **11,924.4** | **12,039.5** | **14,980.2** |

Source: Weglokoks

## Polish coal exports: coking coal 1996 - 1998 (000 tonnes)

|                | 1996    | 1997    | 1998    |
|----------------|---------|---------|---------|
| Austria        | 192.0   | 49.7    | 19.4    |
| Belgium        | 60.0    | 0.0     | 36.7    |
| Belarus        | 0.0     | 0.0     | 0.0     |
| Brazil         | 567.6   | 188.9   | 287.9   |
| Bulgaria       | 244.1   | 142.5   | 153.3   |
| Czech Republic | 488.3   | 219.7   | 109.5   |
| Denmark        | 2.9     | 13.8    | 16.3    |
| Egypt          | 205.3   | 403.8   | 441.9   |
| Finland        | 682.5   | 978.8   | 818.2   |
| France         | 423.2   | 575.5   | 527.8   |
| Germany        | 183.7   | 170.4   | 107.8   |
| Hungary        | 336.3   | 432.8   | 459.7   |
| Netherlands    | 475.2   | 463.9   | 290.0   |
| Romania        | 147.2   | 58.4    | 9.6     |
| Russia         | 193.1   | 0.0     | 25.4    |
| Serbia         | 28.1    | 9.7     | 0.0     |
| Slovak Republic| 731.8   | 303.6   | 452.1   |
| Spain          | 107.8   | 181.4   | 187.8   |
| Sweden         | 389.5   | 421.0   | 59.8    |
| Ukraine        | 2,406.1 | 2,026.2 | 1,180.2 |
| UK             | 149.1   | 0.0     | 0.0     |
| **Total**      | **8,013.8** | **6,640.1** | **5,183.4** |

Source: Weglokoks

The table shows that Germany is the largest importer. The United Kingdom imported twice as much in 1998 as in 1997, but this is still less than Denmark imported.

The word Weglokoks derives from the two Polish words *Wegiel* - coal, and *Koks* - coke.

In its promotional literature it states:

'Poland is a relatively young coal mining country. The most dynamic development of the coal industry occurred after the Second World War, resulting in increased production from circa 50 million tonnes to some 190 million tonnes per year. Hence the position of Polish coal on the domestic and foreign markets is different to that of other European coal countries. The Polish coal industry is a modern industry having a good trained and relatively young manpower of technical staff and miners. It has at its disposal a good research, design and machine back up and support team, which enables this sector to be quite independent in the development of mining.

Due to the above features Polish coal has been - just from the beginning of the post war period - an energy source for most of the European and many overseas countries. It has become a tradition: a prompt and flexible adjustment of coal supplies to the requirements of coal importing markets, especially when energy crises occur, helping to achieve more energy safety in the world.' (Sic)

The Weglokoks brochure continues by lauding the transport facilities. Northwards, coal is delivered to the ports of Szczecin and Gdansk by 'an electrified double track railway equipped with up-to-date installation to provide maximum safety, enabling an increase of velocity of trains to 100 km/hour.'

Southwards, 'By rail, coal is exported to neighbouring countries i.e. Austria, Czech Republic, Slovakia, Germany, Romania, Russia, Ukraine, and to ex Yugoslavia.'

It would of course be surprising if a Weglokoks promotional brochure did anything other than promote, but as Senator Markowski told me, the cost of transporting the coal to the Baltic ports is nearly as great as the cost of mining it.

The International Energy Authority in their 1998 Coal Information Document has produced a breakdown of costs, which shows that Polish coal cannot compete with Australian or South African coal, which is generally US$19 per tonne free on board at Rotterdam.

Polish Coal, Price per Tonne
Pit head price US$15
Transport to Baltic Port US$12
Stevedoring at Baltic Port US$4
Freight via Panamax vessel to Rotterdam US$5
**Total US$36**

Thus a subsidy of US$17 per tonne is needed to bring Polish coal down to the world price.

It breaks EU law to import subsidised coal into any member country, including the UK. For this reason the largest coal mining company in the UK, RJB Mining, is taking the Poles to court, charging them with coal dumping. There are specific peculiarities in the UK. For instance, retired miners in Co. Durham are guaranteed free coal for life. Nowadays this is imported Polish coal.

There is a particular problem with Blue Circle Cement. Cement companies are heavy energy users. Poles are managing to deliver coal to this company at US$50 per tonne at the factory gates. We cannot supply British coal at less than US$130 a tonne.

The Commission in Brussels told me that we should be grateful to the Polish taxpayer for supplying the United Kingdom with nice cheap coal. True enough, but Poland is contravening EU regulations and by so doing she is not helping her accession process at all.

There is already an EU aid programme for Eastern Europe, known by the acronym PHARE.

This sort of aid is at risk if the Poles do not keep to the rules. Indeed in 1998 some US$40 million of PHARE[1] funding was withheld by the Commission's Directorate DGIA (now called DG Enlarge) because the Poles had not abided by its terms and conditions. There is a story doing the rounds in Brussels, possibly apocryphal, that Leszek Balcerowicz telephoned DGIA after this massive penalty and congratulated them on making the right decision.

Be that as it may, the Polish hard coal industry is subsidised by the Commission to the tune of US$20 million per annum. Member countries will be reluctant to continue this if the coal dumping continues.

---

1 *Pologne, Hongrie Assistance a la Recondition Economique.* This fund was originally aimed at Poland and Hungary alone but now helps all eleven countries seeking admission to the European Union.

# CHAPTER 5

## Coal for Heat

Polish coal finds its main customer in the power stations hooked up to the National Grid, but there are also several million small customers who are simply burning coal in open fires.

There is no clean air act in Poland similar to that passed in the UK in 1957, so the worst offender regarding atmospheric pollution is the Polish householder. It is the thousands of ordinary chimneys in town and country that account for most of the particulate emissions that blacken the land. Furthermore, there is a greater temperature range in the East. Krakow's normal range stretches from 32 degrees centigrade in summer to minus 25 in winter.

It has been said that Poland's air would be as clean as ours if this source of pollution ceased, but there are practical problems.

Firstly it is always harder to enforce control on several million small culprits than on a few dozen large ones. Secondly, the open fire is cheap. Heat used to be free under the Communists. Today it is not, but domestic coal is subsidised at around US$4 a tonne, which is less than the subsidy on exported coal but nevertheless significant.

Kym Anderson of the University of Adelaide reasons that it is quite inappropriate for any Government to subsidise a polluting fuel when it should be taxing it. But Governments the world over do subsidise coal. He believes that they act from some death wish to subsidise a dying industry. He cites farming as another example, and the EU's Common Agricultural Policy. Incidentally, Polish farming is so inefficient that it will be the biggest barrier to accession to the EU, but that is outside the scope of this book.[1]

Thus the Poles heat their homes inefficiently with a fuel producing particulates, $SO_2$ and Nox.

There is now clean coal technology for small users called R-2 and marketed by Czysta Polska. R-2 is a smokeless fuel produced from bituminous coal. It will be marketed under the brand name Ekopal. It is light, clean, easy to light and burns entirely pollution-free. It will cost more than coal but less than coke.

The plants making this fuel are relatively expensive at US$25 million for each unit, producing 360,000 tonnes of fuel per year.

I do question the extent of pollution in the plants themselves. My source for this information is Mr Ian Hume of Ian Hume Investments: the company that owns Czysta Polska.

Those who live in flats will have central heating. The boilers that I have seen which heat the water are of primitive design. A simple change which introduces the coal at the bottom rather than the top of the furnace would improve the situation, but such designs cost more.

There is no measurement of delivered heat, nor of heat consumed. Rather, customers are charged by the floor area of their dwellings. This leads to overheated buildings.

The central heating water is corrosive. It attacks the joints in the pipework so hot water and steam leak out. Worse, it corrodes

---

1 Anderson, 'The Political Economies of Coal Subsidies in Europe' from *Energy Policy* special issue June 1995.

valves and thermostats. Therefore none are fitted and the householder can only control the temperature by opening the window.

Corrosion merits its own paragraph. The water is very salty. This is because it has been used to wash sulphur out of the coal at the mines. Polish coal must have its sulphur removed and it is unfortunate that it is also saturated with salt and that this enters the river system.

The Vistula is saltier than the Baltic Sea.

Yet should Poland switch to a cleaner fuel I have it from Senator Markowski that an abandoned coal-mine would put more salt into the system than a working mine. So there is no obvious solution.

The blight of salt water also affects the larger district heating schemes which are common in Polish cities. It is common to have a district plant heating, say, the whole of Sosnowiec or Gliwice. The huge rusty heating pipes are a standard feature of the Polish urban landscape. Very often these plants provide power as well and they are therefore called Combined Heat and Power plants (CHP).

I must here declare an interest as former President of the UK CHP Association and in so doing highlight the myth that CHP provides electrical power more efficiently than a conventional station. The argument runs that a normal station runs at around 30% efficiency but that a CHP station manages 80 or 90%. That is true, but only if one includes the heat element. In theory each unit of heat put in equals the same amount of heat taken out. That is, 100% efficiency.

But each unit of heat put in does not equal the same amount of electricity taken out. Rather, it is around a quarter, and this has little to do with the efficiency of the system. It has more to do with the second law of thermodynamics. The only way to achieve 100% efficiency would be to reduce the temperature of the coolant to absolute zero, which is not possible.

Therefore the higher the ratio of heat/power generation, the higher the efficiency. A CHP plant in Poland, or anywhere, is likely to appear more efficient in mid-winter than in summer, as the ratio of heat to power will be greater. For this reason the most efficient type of CHP plant is that which generates process heat, as the demand for that will be constant the year round.

Readers might find it surprising that a President of CHP should criticise his own industry.

I can only say that on appointment I made my views known to David Green, the Director, and he replied that I was just the type of person they needed! CHP is full of surprises.

The next surprise is less pleasant. It is that the heat to heat conversion rate in Poland is not 100% as it should be, but only 55%. That is due to the many leaks and lack of insulation throughout the system. To give a comparison: in Poland the water leaves the CHP station at 100 degrees centigrade and comes back at 55 degrees. In Denmark I saw it leave the station at 96 degrees and return at 89. That is the heat lost over a considerable distance. At Hoening in Jutland the loop of pipe involved was 60km.

Greater efficiency involves not only system repair but also investment in more efficient boilers. The overall cost of modernising the CHP system is reckoned to be around US$10 billion. Modernisation of district heating plants creates opportunities for large US companies. The World Bank lent Poland US$120 million to modernise the heating systems in Warsaw, Gdansk, Gdynia, Krakow and Katowice.

The next surprise is that Western companies are buying these peculiar Polish hybrids, although they still steer clear of conventional hard coal power stations. This is because a CHP station is part of a separate system. It is an entity. I would argue that it is really a district heating station with some electrical spin off.

I met with Piotr Kolodziej of the Upper Silesian Power Distribution Company in the spring of 1999. The name, incidentally, is misleading as this company's business is not confined to Silesia. He informed me that there were 13 CHP stations due to be privatised. These are: Zielonagora, Torun, Wybrzeze, Tychy, Bedzin,Wroclaw, Gdansk and Bialystok. Also the following: Zeran, Powisle, Kaweczyn, Pruskow I and II, which all heat Warsaw. The various Warsaw stations and Gdansk are World Bank funded, as mentioned above. Bialystok is PHARE funded.

In every case the intention is for employee participation in privatisation. 15% of the stock will go to the workforce free of charge.

At the same meeting Kolodziej's deputy Halima Buk told me that the original plan was to privatise the entire energy sector by 1992, but that this was 'more declaration than practice'.

Electricité de France has now bought a majority shareholding in the CHP plant at Leg, Krakow. The actual breakdown is:

55%      Electricité de France
30%      Government
15%      Employees.

Employees can sell their shares after two years.

Electricité de France has reduced the workforce from 1,350 to 800.

Leg has an installed capacity of 1,454 MW thermal and 452 MW electric.

Power Units 1 and 2 have a rated output of 120 MWE or 158 Mwt.

Power Units 3 and 4 have a rated output of 106 MWE or 196 Mwt.

There are six additional power units which are heat only. One of them produces 70 Mwt and the other five 140 Mwt each.

This reinforces my assertion that CHP plants are primarily district heating plants

I visited Leg in both 1997 and 1999. That is, before and after privatisation. The station shown to me by Jean Michel Mazalerat in 1999 was state of the art and unrecognisable from the station I had seen two years earlier.

M. Mazalerat told me that they had made a small profit on their first year's trading, 12 million zlotys on a turnover of between 300 and 400 million zlotys.

# CHAPTER 6

## Gas

Only 9% of Poland's energy comes from gas because Poland herself has rather small reserves. However gas is a fuel so much cleaner then coal that it seems inevitable that Poland must switch to gas to meet the terms of EU Accession. This will mean importing, principally from the East. Combustion of natural gas does not generate sulphur dioxide or particulates. Emissions of carbon dioxide are 20 to 60% lower than in coal combustion.

It is interesting, first, to describe the extent of all Polish indigenous gas reserves. In 1998 they totalled 150 billion cubic metres (BCM). In that year Poland consumed 11.89 BCM of which 4.78 was domestic and 7.11 imported.

Regarding the domestic reserves, there are:

1. Western deposits described as low methane. These have their own transmission system of 3104 km. They are not connected to the high-pressure methane system of the Eastern deposits.

2. Eastern deposits which are high methane and therefore compatible with the high methane gases imported from the East: that is, they can share the same network of gas mains. The system stretches for 13,109 km and does indeed connect with those of Belarus and the Ukraine, known respectively as the Northern Lights and the Brotherhood pipelines.

3. Coke oven gas, also called Towns Gas. Once common in Silesia this is now being phased out and only represents 1% of

total domestic gas production. There are now only 367 km of pipeline.

4. Coal bed methane. The reserves are estimated to be very high: 100 BCM in Silesia alone and one trillion CM nation-wide. Various companies have bought concessions for coal bed methane exploration. They include Amoco, Elektrogaz Ventures and McCormick.

However, according to the United States Department of Energy, 'Production costs are relatively high and the full economic potential is still to be assessed.'

Until the Energy Law of 1997 all gas, whether domestic or foreign, was controlled by the Polish Oil and Gas Company (POGC). This was one of the last fully integrated hydrocarbon monopolies in Europe. I will return to oil later on. But so far as gas was concerned, POGC controlled all of the following:

1. Exploration, development and operation of deposits.
2. Construction and operation of transmission and distribution systems.
3. Construction and operation of underground storage facilities.
4. Surface and drilling geophysics.
5. Design, manufacture and repair of machinery.
6. Production, distribution and transmission of gas.
7. Rescue work.
8. Vocational training.
9. Hotel trade.
10. Gas imports.
11. Gas exports.
12. Sale of motor vehicles.
13. Domestic and foreign trade.
14. Operation of customs depots.

In 1997 the Polish Office for Competition and Customer Protection required POGC to reduce its share in newly established companies to below 50%. This requirement was reinforced by:

1. Poland's 1997 Energy Law which specifies a free market in gas. 'Gas undertakings which engage in gas transmission and distribution are obliged to provide transmission services to all entities if the gas is produced in Poland'.

2. Poland's adoption of the Gas Directive by the European Parliament on 22 June 1998 and acceleration of gas sector liberalisation.

POGC reacted to these laws with an amended sequence of objectives, as follows:

1. Separation of gas transmission.
2. Formation of gas distribution companies based on the assets of POGC gas units.
3. Pilot privatisation of 2 or 3 distribution companies.
4. Privatisation of the remaining distribution companies.
5. Formation of production companies.

This process should be completed by 2002. POGC cost it at US$57 billion.

I met Wieslaw Prugar, the Director of Polish Oil and Gas, in the summer of 2000. To my surprise I discovered that his perception is not that his monopoly will be broken: rather that Polish Oil and Gas will be changed into a holding company with numerous daughter companies. Therefore the five separate functions mentioned would be mere operating companies controlled by the main company based in Warsaw.

Surely item 4; 'Privatisation of the remaining distribution companies' is quite incompatible with this structure?

Mr Prugar explained that should POGC be broken up into quite separate companies they would then be far too weak to compete with the Russian gas export giant Gazprom. In particular he did not see how separate companies would have the power to negotiate import deals with other countries such as Norway.

The day before we had met with the regulator, Mr Juchniewicz. He has different views on the break up of POGC. The companies will indeed be quite independent. He is keen to diversify supply and sees no difficulty in importing Norwegian gas: up to half a billion cubic metres of it each year. The only difficulty at present is one of gas prices in general, which are rising by 12.5% a year, well above the inflation rate. The heating element of the Polish family budget is far higher than in Western Europe. It is therefore very important to reduce gas prices, the more so since the regulator wishes to switch ordinary people from coal to gas. He sees completely independent companies working in a competitive market as the solution. Even the Polish Oil and Gas Company is forecasting an increase in gas for heating from 5.4 billion cubic metres in 1996 to 9 billion in 2010. In addition to this huge switch in the domestic sector, Juchniewicz anticipates a threefold increase in the use of gas for electricity generation by 2020.

Another notable omission from the above laws and programme is the denial of free access to the gas network of foreign gas. This too is believed to be caused by POGC's fear that the Russians and their massive company Gazprom would completely dominate the market. However this denial of access does not accord with the EU Gas Directive mentioned above and therefore makes a slight nonsense of Poland's adoption of it.

Third-party access (TPA) is a prerequisite of the gas directive. The regulator's assistant, Dr Miroslaw Duda, told us, 'It is quite simple. The night before we join the EU we switch over to third-party access'. It is possible that Polish Oil and Gas might be able to change to a form of negotiated TPA, but even this will involve considerable restructuring and cannot take less than two years.

A foreign company can access the Polish Gas Grid if the field it is developing is in Poland.

On January 25, 2000, the Texan oil company Apache announced 'First discovery in Poland. Well produces 16.9 million cubic feet of gas per day'. They were referring to their Wilga Well, in block 225 of the Vistula Concession, 25 miles South East of Warsaw. Apache currently has 11.5 million acres under lease in Poland with options on another 3.4 million acres.

The present system has 17,000 kilometres of high-pressure gas transmission pipelines and 87.5 thousand kilometres of lower pressure distribution lines. The system supplies 4,000 localities, including 530 towns, where gas is used by 6.7 million households. Some 100,000 new customers are connected to the network each year.

All of the above gas production forecasts exclude the power sector.

There are signs that gas is making inroads into coal's traditional domain. I see mentioned by POGC, 'Boilers and district heating schemes in health resorts where preservation of the environment is particularly important.' These are merely 'planned', but one can reasonably assume that gas as fuel might spread from district heating plants to Combined Heat and Power Plants, because a CHP plant is normally located in a densely populated area.

Indeed, there are several projects under way to develop gas fired CHPs. They include Nowa Sarzyna (Enron) and Zamosc (Southern Electric). Another will be built in Zarnowiec on the site of the old nuclear station by an American company bearing the interesting name 'AES Electric and Failure Analysis'. Other CHP stations under conversion are at Gorzow and the two due to be privatised at Bialystok and Gdynia. The most important is the coal gas conversion planned for half the units of the 1,800 MW Polaniec power station, to which I will return in the power station chapter.

Fluctuations in gas demand are considerable. 19 million cubic metres are used in summer: 45 million during the winter peak. This raises problems of security of supply. In consequence, gas must be stored in underground holders: usually old salt mines or depleted gas deposits in the lowlands and sub-Carpathian regions.

These subterranean gasometers require constant and costly investment. Present storage capacity is only 0.7 billion cubic metres but the Poles hope to increase this to 4.5 billion by 2010. Present storage facilities, with start up dates, are:

Brzeznica, 1979.
Swarzow, 1979.
Strachocina, 1982.
Husow, 1987.

The most remarkable and largest is Wierzchowice. This was an active gas field until 1 April 1995. Only 53 days after closure, the gas started to flow to storage in the opposite direction.

In the heavy frosts of 1996/7 Wierzchowice was supplying 7% of daily domestic gas demand.

The Poles also hire underground storage space from the Ukraine.

There is also gas in the Baltic. There are four concentrations, around 50 miles north of Rozewie, which is Poland's northernmost cape. Deposits discovered so far only amount to 7 billion cubic metres. These are being exploited by the Polish firm Petrobaltic. It has only been drilling since 1992. It is the sole company in the Baltic with sufficient equipment, experience and staff for extracting gas. The company plans to expand its activities to include the exploration of oil deposits near Kaliningrad.

It is evident that the Poles are attempting a coal to gas switch but this is being hindered by the existing monopolistic Polish Oil and Gas Company.

There are also the coal-miners, fearful of losing their jobs.

### Liquified Petroleum Gas

This is almost entirely imported from Russia, Germany, Belarus, Slovakia, Norway and Lithuania. Distributors are BP Gas, Baltyk Gas, Gaspol, Elektrim-Europgaz, Shell Gas, Petroenergogaz and Topgas. The market is quite large; 4.5 million Polish households use it, compared to the 6.5 million who use mains gas. No licence is needed to trade it and gas cylinders produced by small distributors often do not comply with safety standards and explode.

In addition 350,000 cars run on LPG, including 60% of the taxis in Poland's largest cities.

The Polish LPG market is the fastest growing of any LPG market in Europe. It stood at 690,000 tonnes in 1996 and is reckoned to be 1.2 million tonnes by 2000.

## Eastern Gas

As the Soviet Union set about industrialising its satellites in Eastern Europe, it connected them to the huge gas fields of Kazakhstan and Turkmenistan. Indeed not only were countries such as Czechoslovakia, Hungary and the Baltic States terminals for Soviet Gas pipelines, they were also transit countries through which that gas was exported to Western Europe. Gas was an important earner of hard currency.

But Poland was bypassed. The Soviets reckoned that Poland did not herself need gas as she had so much coal. Thus the main pipelines went south, through the Ukraine via Czechoslovakia to the West, and also via Estonia to Scandinavia. Poland was supplied through the Brotherhood and Northern Lights spurs already mentioned. However, these supply routes alone provided more gas than Poland did domestically, 7 BCM per annum compared to 4 BCM.

The break up of the Soviet Union and a discovery of a colossal gas field in the Yamal Peninsula in Western Siberia changed that.

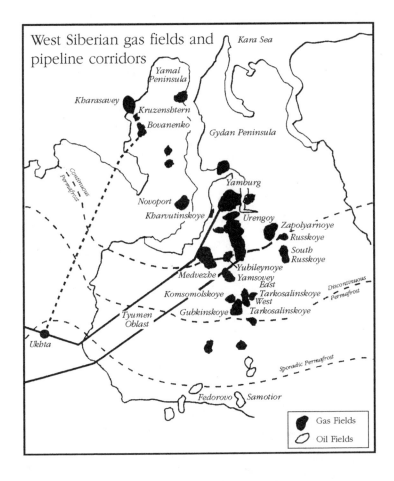

West Siberian gas fields and pipeline corridors

Kara Sea

Yamal Peninsula

Kharasavey

Kruzenshtern

Bovanenko

Gydan Peninsula

Continuous Permafrost

Yamburg

Novoport

Kharvutinskoye

Urengoy

Zapolyarnoye

Russkoye

South Russkoye

Yubileynoye

Medvezhe

Yamsovey East

Komsomolskoye

Tarkosalinskoye

West Tarkosalinskoye

Discontinuous Permafrost

Tyumen Oblast

Gubkinskoye

Ukhta

Sporadic Permafrost

Fedorovo

Samotior

Gas Fields

Oil Fields

Regarding the break up, Russia found herself in difficulties carrying gas through the Ukraine. The Ukrainians could not pay the Russians for the gas that they themselves used. Russia, naturally, shut down those pipelines terminating in the Ukraine, but this was a Pyrrhic victory since Ukraine then siphoned off gas from the West European pipelines. Russia, fearful of losing its reputation as a reliable supplier to the West, was then forced to re-open the Ukrainian lines.

The new northern gas fields have been found to be at least ten times the size of the southern ones. The Siberian field is north of the Arctic Circle on the Gydan peninsula and near the island of Nova Zemlya. It lies in permafrost. The Russians aim to export an additional 60 billion cubic metres a year from this northern field. In so doing they will depress gas prices throughout Europe.

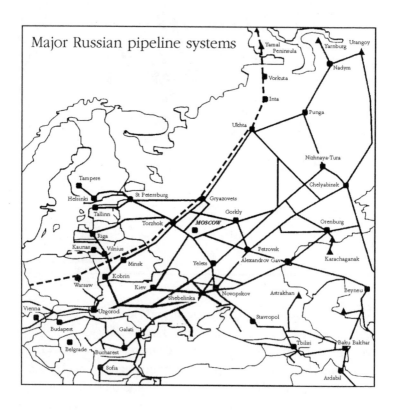

The entire cost of the Yamal line is reckoned to be US$35 billion. The Polish sector will run from Kondratki, on the border with Belorus, to the German border town of Gorzyca. It will carry 65.7 BCM. Two parallel lines are planned, each of 665 km. The first was scheduled to become operational in 1999 whilst the second will not be completed until 2010. Some forecasts estimate a Polish gas demand of between 22 and 27 billion BCM by 2010.

That being so, and due to a Polish fear of having all its eggs in one Russian basket, the present Government is making efforts to diversify.

As mentioned above, Poland and Norway signed an agreement in 1999 for 500 million cubic metres. This could rise to 2.5 billion cubic metres via a pipeline through Germany built by Poland's Bartimpex and Germany's Ruhrgas. A second German pipeline is planned by Verbundnetz.

A pipeline under the Baltic is also under consideration, should Polish demand develop to warrant such an expensive scheme. Finally, the Dutch company Gasunie is seeking a deal with Poland similar to Norway's. However, Gasunie would be selling Russian gas: that is, the supply would be guaranteed by the Dutch but would originate in Russia. This would not therefore contribute to Poland's goal of diversification.

Indeed the European Union is a net importer of gas, so the whole alliance will rely on the fields of Turkmenistan, Kazakhstan and Western Siberia as main suppliers. Additional imports will come from North Africa.

## Coal to Gas Substitution Schemes

With such huge reserves of gas all around her it is perhaps surprising that Poland still derives 76% of her primary energy from coal. This compares with a European Union average of between 25 and 40%.

The coal mining lobby is still very strong, and Polish coal is subsidised, whereas Polish gas is not. With the passing of the 1997 Energy Law the new regulator, Juchniewicz, has the power to control electricity and gas prices, but he cannot control the price charged to the power stations by the coal-mines.

The Government will set maximum consumer prices for ordinary coal fired boilers and open fires: but should these prices be exceeded by the cost of production the Government will make good the shortfall by reimbursing the coal-mines. Thus coal still enjoys a privileged position in both heat and power sectors.

Coal is particularly uncompetitive in medium sized boilers of between 5 and 50 megawatts thermal and even more so in small boilers below 5 Mwt.

Thus there are substitution schemes for this end of the market. The Global Environmental Facility, a special UN fund, has contributed US$25 million through the World Bank with these objectives:

1. To stimulate self-replicable technological and institutional changes that would promote coal to gas substitution in small to medium sized boilers and induce more energy efficient practices in the operation and design of new residential buildings.

2. To demonstrate substitution and improve the overall energy efficiency throughout the heat supply chain as a means of reducing carbon dioxide emissions.

In 1990 George Bush, then the President of the USA, visited Krakow bringing about the decision of the US Congress to vote US$20 million for 'activities aimed at reduction of emission sources.'

Generally the switch from coal to gas has been somewhat sluggish. Gas production has risen from 4.2 billion to 5.04 billion cubic metres over the past decade, and consumption from 11.2 billion to 13.02. These statistics are from the US Energy Administration, August 1999.

## Other Fuel and Power Sources

### Oil

This important energy source is mainly used for transport and therefore is strictly outside the scope of this book.

However the number of road vehicles is doubling every five years. Thus environmental improvements caused by a switch to gas and a cleaner coal technology are likely to be cancelled out by Poland's explosion of road traffic.

Oil was the sole province of the Polish Oil and Gas Company, until the energy law of 1997. There is now a free market in oil.

Poland only produces 1.3% of her oil requirements. That is, 5,000 barrels per day (bbd) out of a consumption of 425,000 bbd, leaving 420,000 bbd to be imported. Therefore Poland's principal activity lies in refining this oil which she does at Petrochemica Plock: 260,000 bbd, and Rafineria Gdansk, 90,000 bbd. This leaves a shortfall of 75,000 bbd which Poland must import in its refined state.

**Hydro**

Poland is a flat country, so the amount of hydro is not significant. There are some reservoirs in the Tatra mountains. These mark the border between Poland and Slovakia.

True hydro accounts for 1.14% of total power generation, whilst pumped storage accounts for a little more: 2%.

Only 19% of the economic potential from hydro is used by Poland, so this would indicate a full potential of around 15%, including pumped storage. Whilst this is very useful load following plant it is not clean, as electricity is needed to pump the water back up the hill.

**Nuclear**

I have already mentioned the power station at Zarnowiec which was half built and abandoned at the time of the Chernobyl disaster. It was to be of 465 MWE. Before that two other stations had been planned, one of which was near Warta.

The AWS states that 'The option to launch a nuclear programme has been deferred by Government until 2007.'

**Green**

There is no significant green lobby in Poland.

Professor Kassenberg of the Institute for Sustainable Development in Warsaw wishes to develop hay boilers and Dr Adam Gula of the Polish Foundation for Energy Efficiency believes that there is future for straw boilers. Both these systems are $CO_2$ neutral: that is, as much carbon dioxide is fixed by the growing crop as is released by the burning crop in the boiler. These fuels require small on-site power stations. Transporting them any distance would create $CO_2$ problems much greater than those caused by coal as the thermal efficiency of hay and straw is low and huge amounts would be needed to power a station of say 2,000 megawatts. Therefore the whole structure of power stations would have to be changed should the use of these fuels become common. Small is beautiful but also very expensive.

There are a few wind turbines on the Baltic Coast already connected to the grid. They are not significant compared to German wind turbines. These generate 100 times the power of the Polish machines.

It would be quite simple for Poland to increase her wind power, but in general the country does not seem particularly interested in renewable energy.

She has a target of 8% but not until 2020 AD.

Coal is still king.

# CHAPTER 7

## The Lignite Story

Poland has one other source of power so separate that I have saved it until last. This is lignite.

Lignite provides about a quarter of Poland's power; 8,500 megawatts. It is in three huge deposits, none of them in Silesia. The Belchatow deposit is south of Lodz, the Turow deposit is in the extreme south west in the oddly named Zittau Bag and the Patnow-Adamov-Konin deposit, PAK for short, is 200 km west of Warsaw. (PAK is somewhat complicated. It has three power stations supplied by two mines that are part of the Konin Turek brown coal basin, 30 km apart.)

Lignite has a reputation as a dirty fuel. Actually it is no dirtier than black coal, but it has only two fifths of black coal's calorific value. Therefore two and a half times as much lignite is needed to generate one unit of power. Lignite is also known as brown coal, but the Polish lignite looks black. I suggest that brown coal's bad reputation stems not from the Polish deposits but from those in the neighbouring countries: the Czech Republic and the New German Länder. But of course, with the lower calorific value, all problems of aerial pollution must be multiplied by two and a half, whichever country is producing the lignite.

Lignite pollution differs from hard coal pollution in these ways:

1. Atmospheric. Emissions of dust, $SO_2$, Nox and $CO_2$ are greater due to the greater tonnage of lignite needed to produce an equal amount of power.

2. Aquatic. Lignite does not need to be washed so there is no discharge of salt to the rivers.

3. Terrestrial. Worse, as lignite mines are open cast. They are more of an eyesore than deep mines. The Poles seek to alleviate the problem by the replacement of overburden, top soil and then afforestation of worked out areas.

The Poles are taking measures to clean up lignite emissions, which naturally raise the cost of lignite power, but it is still nowhere near the cost of hard coal power. One visit to a lignite mine will show why.

A lignite mine is simply a hole in the ground. That at Turow is of 20,000 acres. PAK is about the same, and Belchatow 30,000. Turow and PAK are surface deposits but Belchatow is 80 metres down.

Thus anything to do with lignite is big. Bucket excavators on tracks crawl along the coal faces scooping lignite directly onto conveyor belts that lead straight to the furnaces. These excavators weigh around 1,000 tonnes apiece. The process is continuous throughout the year, for the lignite plants are producing Poland's base load electricity. The process appears wholly automated but actually it is not. There are miners: 6,000 in the case of Belchatow. At Turow 12,000 jobs depend on the mine and power station.

Nevertheless brown coal is not as labour intensive as black coal. To state the obvious; open cast is not as labour intensive as deep mined coal.

Poland's base load is generated by a mere three power stations.

1. Turow produces 2 gigawatts.

2. PAK 2.73 gigawatts (of which, Patnow 1600 MW, Adamov 600 MW, Konin 583 MW).

3. Belchatow generates 4.32 gigawatts. This makes Belchatow the biggest power station in Europe. Its two chimneys are as tall as the Eiffel Tower. All three lignite stations are bigger than any hard coal station in Poland.

The turbine hall at Belchatow is so long that I could not see one end from the other. Edward Najgebauer, the Managing Director, showed me his array of 12 x 360 megawatt turbines disappearing into the distance and said 'The most important aspect of lignite power is that it is unsubsidised'. This is indeed right. Ironically however, Poland's efforts to comply with EU directives and Kyoto are making lignite power more expensive. The standard method of cleaning up sulphur dioxide is by wet flue gas desulphurisation (FGD). Limestone is injected into the gases which absorbs the $SO_2$ and combines with it to form gypsum, a useful building material. Nitrous oxide is removed by the fitting of low Nox burners. These two techniques are expensive, particularly if retrofitted. It is thus more accurate to say that lignite power used to be unsubsidised.

Belchatow now has six of its twelve turbine units fitted with flue gas desulphurisation. It has been able to fund this by agreeing a higher selling price for its electricity with the Polish Power Grid. The contract is for 15 years. It is one of the main problems facing Juchniewicz, the regulator. By the nature of his job he is at daggers drawn with the lignite power stations which are now being told to clean up their act whilst maintaining the same prices. Juchniewicz's remit is to obtain the lowest price for the end user.

What hope is there, one might ask, that Belchatow retrofits FGD on the remaining six turbine units? The surprising answer is 'Plenty. The Japanese and the French and Britain's National Power are competing to build a second power station at Belchatow, of 800 megawatts' (Najgebauer). This is to cover the shortfall in generation whilst the remaining units are shut down two at a time for FGD conversion.

Lignite power is an attractive investment for the West even including the costly environmental requirements. On the other hand, it is harder to be positive if neighbouring countries and Polish lignite history are taken into account.

It was Stalin, the man of coal and steel, who decided that lignite mining should be hugely increased after the Second World War. The Poles had the most mining experience. Therefore the Poles should build the mines and power stations in East Germany, Czechoslovakia and Poland itself. This they did to a uniform design. Installations built totalled around a dozen each in Germany and Czechoslovakia and the three already mentioned in Poland. The main concentration was in the Bohemian Basin. By 1989 the pollution was quite appalling and the area came to be called the 'black triangle'. It contains the notorious dead forest.

After 1989 the Czech Republic took some 'remedial measures'. Germany closed down its dirtiest lignite mines. It seems odd that the Poles did not make the same decision. That is, unless Polish lignite is less polluting than East German or Czech lignite.

Actually, the Germans are opening a new lignite mine, but in the West. This is cheap, clean lignite and despite a battle with the Greens, the Westfalian Government has the go ahead. So the key factor must be the quality of the lignite.

# Emissions from Lignite Power Stations
## (in thousands of tonnes)

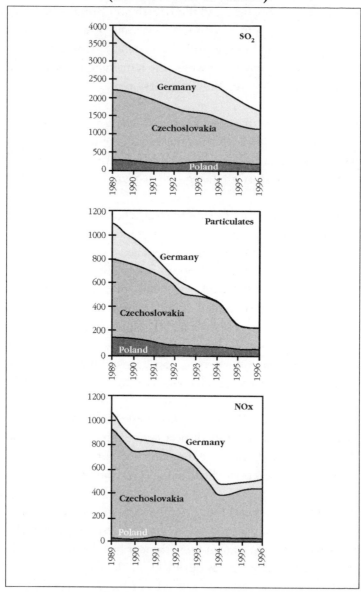

In 1998 I went to the centre of the black triangle where PHARE have a monitoring unit at Usti on the Elbe. The triangle is no longer black. It is a green lush valley. At that stage there were few German mines but many Czech. These were all small scale compared with Turow some 100 yards over the Polish Border. That Turow is in Poland occupying a narrow peninsula is due to the quirks of the Oder Neisse line. The River Neisse runs just a few yards to the west of the Turow 20,000 acre hole. Incidentally its level is higher than the bottom of this gigantic basin and it is lucky that the whole of Turow was not flooded in the great storms of July 98, which were violent enough to bring down the old Communist Government.

Be that as it may, the international situation in the black triangle is such that the Czechs and the Germans are blaming the Poles for pollution. Josef Kozlowski, head of the power station at Turow, thinks this a bit rich since the prevailing wind is southwest and the bulk of the gases blow over Poland.

I obtained from PHARE the graphs reproduced opposite which show beyond a peradventure that the Czechs are the main polluters, at least until 1996.

However the Poles have clearly taken notice of international feelings, for their measures to clean up the Turow emissions are so sophisticated that they make anything done at Belchatow seem like a bargain basement.

Turow has ten units, each of 200 MW. It is installing fluidised beds in six of them, built by Foster Wheeler. The beds are of sand heated by combustion gases. The Turow beds will be the biggest in the world. The official reason for this costly solution is that there is no room for wet FGD: that is, the type of FGD that produces gypsum from limestone. Turow is fitting dry FGD in another 3 units. This produces less useful by-products but takes up less room. One unit is to be closed down.

Returning to the costly fluidised beds these sophisticated animals are uniquely good at burning poor fuels, such as printers' sludge or anthracite culm. Thus it is possible that Kozlowski did a good PR job on me in assuring me that the lignite at Turow was of the highest quality. It may be poor stuff. It is also possible that Foster Wheeler are using the Poles as guinea pigs and that they do not really need fluidised beds. It is true that there is very little room. A few steps one way and you're in Germany. A few steps the other and you're in the Czech Republic.

The principal advantage of the fluidised bed is that it burns coal more efficiently and thereby reduces $CO_2$ emissions as well as $SO_2$ and Nox.

Turow is unique amongst Polish power complexes in that it is still an arm of the Department of Energy. It is not a joint stock company. This could account for the feasibility of paying for the fluidised beds. However, Turow did achieve a special selling price to the Power Grid, which is just about double the average price, and, worse, this is another long-term contract and another headache for Juchniewicz the regulator.

I save the most surprising Turow fact until last. Westerners are now interested in buying a share in it. The power plant is being supported by the consortium of the World Bank, BRE Bank and Pekao SA. Thus even the most expensive lignite complex seems attractive to the West. It does strike me that, provided the fuel is of high quality, lignite is in a different league from deep mined hard coal.

Events at PAK support this. The West already has a 20% stake in it. PAK was the scene of the great battle in 1999 between National Power and Elektrim. Elektrim, a Polish American Consortium, won. (National Power could not agree a satisfactory long-term sales contract.)

Thus the West has an interest in all the lignite stations: PAK, Turow and Belchatow.

Elsewhere, the West has bought in to some combined heat and power stations (listed in Chapter 5) which are peripheral to the main power network. The West only has one 25% stake in one of the 33 mainstream hard coal power stations. This is Polaniec, mentioned in the next chapter.

Thus, in the lignite field, we have what appears to be nonsense. Just as the lignite producers raise their prices the West becomes interested in buying them.

There is one further complication. The lignite prices are being raised because of money spent on sulphur dioxide, nitrous oxide and particulate emissions. The decisions to spend this money were made by the Poles before the great global warming scare. Flue gas desulphurisation clean-up techniques need power, resulting in a loss of efficiency, resulting in an increase in $CO_2$ emissions. So PAK and Belchatow will in future be producing more $CO_2$ (or less power). This is bad news on the climate change front, but it is probably within maxima decided at Kyoto as with a base line of 1990 and the subsequent collapse of heavy industry Poland has a $CO_2$ credit which she can either use or sell as tradeable permits. Turow alone will actually decrease its $CO_2$ emissions by fitting fluidised beds.

The average Pole, brought up as Homo Sovieticus, would have seen much sense in Stalin's coal mining expansion of the late 40s and early 50s. It was a good old Victorian Concept. 'Where there's muck there's money'. He would understand the old slogan on Turow's stacks, 'We will smoke on time'.

But Homo Sovieticus would not have understood the spending of huge sums merely to reduce emissions. He would be mystified by the new Turow slogan which reads, 'We are giving up smoking'.

# CHAPTER 8

## Hard Coal and Electricity

Polish power stations visited

This is the linchpin of this book.

Until 1989 electricity was controlled by the State in all its aspects. There was a wide range of hidden subsidies and electricity was sold at below economic cost.

During 1989 and 1990 came the first indicators of long-term reforms aimed at decentralisation, productivity increase, promotion of competition, privatisation, and de-regulation. The reforms were designed to treat energy as a commodity and to open the sector to capital markets. The reforms started with the disbanding of the amalgamated power and lignite industry enterprises and of five large power engineering regions. This laid the groundwork for commercialisation.

Today the power sector has the following characteristics:

1. There is an over-capacity of electricity generation.
2. Many of the power stations are old and inefficient.
3. Domestic coal fuels the overwhelming majority of electricity generation.
4. There are severe environmental problems.
5. Electricity prices have recently been removed from government control.
6. There is a lack of State finance.
7. Privatisation is only just beginning.

(From *The Electricity Market in Poland* by Michael Davies, a partner of Allen and Overy, UK solicitors with a branch in Warsaw.)

Whilst black coal is the major fuel, lignite produces a greater proportion of the country's electrical needs as it is a base load fuel.

This shows up in these two pie charts opposite.

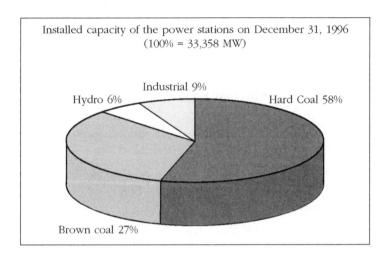

Installed capacity of the power stations on December 31, 1996
(100% = 33,358 MW)

Industrial 9%
Hydro 6%
Hard Coal 58%
Brown coal 27%

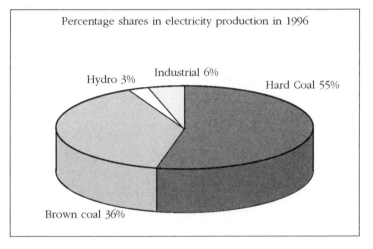

Percentage shares in electricity production in 1996

Hydro 3%
Industrial 6%
Hard Coal 55%
Brown coal 36%

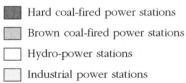

Hard coal-fired power stations
Brown coal-fired power stations
Hydro-power stations
Industrial power stations

Source: "Interim Report on National Power System in 1996". PSE SA.
National Power Control Center, March 1997.

But hard deep mined coal remains the main fuel for the power stations, and it is worth listing these stations, not only to show their installed capacity, but also to show their average age.

## Principal Power Stations

| Station | Installed Capacity (Megawatts) | First year of operation |
|---|---|---|
| Kozineice | 2,600 | 1972 |
| Opole | 2,160 | 1993 |
| Dolna Odra | 1,600 | 1974 |
| Polaniec | 1,600 | 1979 |
| Rybnik | 1,600 | 1972 |
| Jaworzno III | 1,270 | 1996 |
| Laziska | 1,040 | 1967 |
| Lagisza | 840 | 1963 |
| Siersza | 740 | 1962 |
| Ostroleka B | 600 | 1972 |
| Skawina | 550 | 1957 |
| Stalowa Wola | 385 | 1954 |
| Jaworzno II | 350 | 1953 |
| Blachownia | 281 | 1957 |
| Halemba | 200 | 1962 |
| Jaworzno I | 146 | 1938 |
| Pomorzany | 120 | 1960 |
| Miechowice | 110 | 1953 |

Thus the principal power stations have an installed capacity of 17,792 megawatts.

To this total must be added 8,500 MW from the modern lignite power stations already mentioned and 3,700 megawatts from the CHP stations.

Some of the CHP stations are of great age. Eight of them predate World War One and three were built in the late 1880s. Boilers are also ancient. 60% have been operating for more than 15 years and 40% for more than 20. Of the 225 turbine sets 58% are 15 years old and 37% over 30. It is generally reckoned that installations that have worked for more than 17 years are worn out.

The total is 29,992 megawatts installed capacity from coal, which leaves a small balance of 3,000 megawatts to be raised from all other sources, including hydro, to make up the grand total of 33,000 megawatts, with peak demand over recent years never exceeding 23,000 megawatts. The power stations of all types feed into the grid shown on page 102.

The Department of Energy favours an amalgamation of power stations into perhaps five groupings. Only in this way can Polish power compete with the huge companies of Western Europe: National Power and Powergen in England or Electricité de France. This is reminiscent of the hard coal-mine amalgamation and it could be a device for supporting the old and dirty power stations.

Jaworzno II, Laziska, Lagisza, Siersza and Halemba have already merged to form 'The Southern Power Plant Concern'. It is here worth quoting Klemens Scierski who is now Vice President of Laziska power station and was also the Minister for Trade and Industry in the SLD government which fell in 1997.

# Electrical Power System of Poland – Major Plants and Transmission Lines

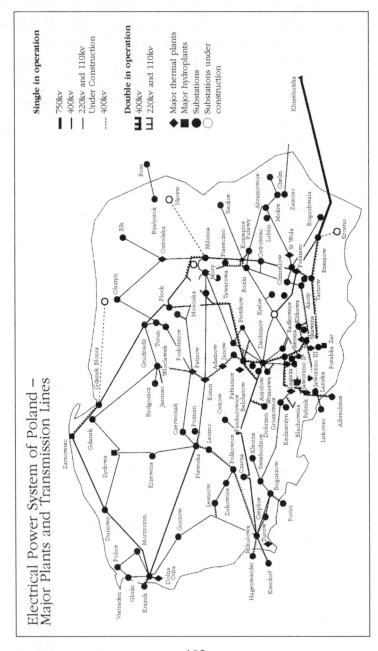

When asked how he assessed the chances of the Polish power sector in comparison to other plants operating in the EU Mr Scierski replied:

'Frankly speaking I cannot imagine a Polish power station with an installed capacity of 2000 MW competing with giants such as Electricité de France, 117,000 MW, or the Italian Enel, 96,000 MW. All power stations in Poland have a total generating capacity of 33,000 megawatts. So two solutions are possible: either 1) Polish power plants will become an integrated part of Western companies or, 2) There will be capital groups set up by electric power companies vertically and horizontally diversified.'

There is a difference though between coal and power. The old coal-mines are producing expensive coal. The old power stations are producing cheap power (albeit polluting).

When I met with the regulator, Mr Juchniewicz, on 19 April 1999 he said:

'There is a 10,000 MW surplus. Generators must close. Ironically the most modern plants should close first, as they are the most expensive.'

Juchniewicz recognises that the cost of building new power stations greatly exceeds that of simply keeping the old ones ticking over. However his statement is not completely correct, as combustion in old power stations is less efficient and the cost per unit of electricity therefore greater. Juchniewicz is criticising the fitting of flue gas desulphurisation units and low Nox burners to new power stations because of the expense. Besides nearly doubling the cost of the build, these clean up techniques use 3% of electricity generated and therefore decrease efficiency by that amount.

He said later, 'Economy is the prime concern of the regulator'. That being so, his ideal power station would burn coal extremely efficiently but would not be cluttered up with environmental frills. His duty is to deliver electricity to customers at minimum prices. He feels that power stations are not doing this. He is supported by Adam Gula of the alternative energy group FEWE (in English, standing for The Polish Foundation for Energy Efficiency), who told me that, 'power stations and coal-mines do not serve the community but dictate to it. They are motivated by the desire for self-aggrandisement.' Also, more cynically, 'competition is bad for the environment'.

Adam Gula believes that the Polish electrical power sector requires an investment of approximately US$50 billion over the next 15 years to satisfy environmental standards and to replace 16 GW of obsolete installed capacity.

The general desire of the Polish Government is to export more power to the West via greater links between the Central European Grid, CENTREL, and the West European Grid, UCPTE. They can only do this by modernising the power sector. At the moment CENTREL fails EU standards on several fronts:
   1. The voltage varies.
   2. The frequency varies.
   3. There is not sufficient security of supply.
   Thus Poland does export, but via the rather complicated device known as a 'Back to Back D/C link'. Poland has been exporting some electricity to UCPTE since 1995.

Poland would wish to sell its worst power stations to the West (Halemba is a notable example of the dirtiest) but not unnaturally the West prefers the best, cleanest stations: those

stations on which the Poles have already spent a lot of money;
Polaniec, Rybnik, Opole and Jaworzno III. I will describe these
in turn.

## Polaniec

The Belgian company Tractabel owns a quarter of this power
station. It is of 1,800 MW and in the middle of nowhere:
equidistant from the Silesian mines and the Bogdanka mine in
Lublin. It is the main user of coal from Bogdanka, a new and
profitable mine, which will itself soon be privatised.

Tractabel owns 25% plus one share, which is all-important as
no policy changes can be made at Polaniec without a 75%
majority. Marek Woloch, the Director, wished to privatise
Polaniec because he was being controlled by PSE's dispatching
centre in Warsaw. His electricity was competitively priced but
the Grid decided to take only 50% of his capacity.

It has eight units, four of them equipped with FGD. $SO_2$
emissions from these are 600 mg per cubic metre, which is
well within limits. From the non-FGD units the emissions were
2,350 mg when I was in the control room. This is just on the
limit borderline. However, Mr Woloch has quite revolutionary
plans for these four units. He plans to convert them to gas.

Polaniec is therefore a unique power station in that it is privately
owned, and soon to be gas powered. Woloch is able to switch
to gas because he is so far away from the mines and the miners.
He is in the depths of the country, and it is remarkable just
how poor this countryside is. I saw farmers with horses working
the same equipment that I just remember from war time Britain.
Rural poverty is the true Polish poverty. Polaniec is the third
biggest employer in the voivodship and contributes 64% of its

income. It will become even bigger when Woloch completes a factory to fabricate gypsum building blocks. It is interesting to speculate how many other power stations might follow Woloch's gas conversion scheme if they were not located in the middle of mining areas.

## Rybnik

Rybnik produces the cheapest power from hard coal in Poland. It is 1,740 MWE: a little smaller than Polaniec, and burns coal that is low in sulphur. It is in the mining area south of Katowice. It has been selected by the State Treasury as suitable for privatisation.

35% is on offer and a consortium of Marubeni, NRG and GE Capital is interested. Should this consortium fail, UK's National Power is waiting in the wings to take up the entire 35%.

The Director of Rybnik, Tadeusz Sopicki, told me that he, like Woloch, felt that his production was under too much central control and that he could perform much better privatised in a free market.

Rybnik's power is cheaper than Polaniec's, but in other respects it is less good. Its boilers are fitted only with dry FGD. This does not produce a useful by-product such as gypsum. Instead it produces ash, which the coal-mines use to infill disused workings. Rybnik must pay the mines for this disposal. Rybnik has no cooling towers. It uses a huge artificial lake, which is a social asset as it never freezes and can be used for sailing the year round. Mr Sopicki feels that when he is privatised he will be able to use his profits on other social assets. In particular he is keen to build a College for Girls. This is a commendable desire but does show that the Director is still thinking on Communist Welfare lines. Marubeni, or National Power, will not wish to spend the profits of this power station on good works.

## Opole

Opole took thirty years to build. It produces the highest cost electricity in Poland.

Its Director, Josef Pekala, signed an agreement with Juio Lopez Castano of the Spanish generating giant Endesa in September 1999.

There is much in its favour.

1. It operates at high temperatures, using supercritical steam (540 degrees Celsius at 170/60 bars) This will reduce $CO_2$ emissions by 20%.

2. The aim is to transport coal by barge. Since rail cost is almost as much as pithead cost this will greatly reduce the price of coal for Opole.

3. The station is developing a district heating scheme for the city of Opole.

4. There is FGD which produces high quality gypsum. The gypsum plant was built in collaboration with the Norwegians. It is the largest in Europe and sells 40 million square metres of plasterboard annually.

5. Opole also sells half a million tonnes of fly ash suitable for road building.

6. The power station is reliable. Its availability is 92%.

Opole's power may be expensive to produce, but this does not mean that the price charged for it is high. Indeed it is in receipt of a considerable Government subsidy which enables it to sell cheaply by special contract.

## Special Contracts

There are a staggering 14.5 million special contracts between generators and customers.

Those customers could be regional electricity companies, or they could be large industries.

This is a legacy of the Communist system, when selling prices were set by Government. In Opole's case the contracts are clearly a boon, but they can equally be a curse. An old, dirty power station will receive little or no subsidy and will therefore have to sell electricity so cheaply that it cannot set aside money to clean up its emissions. With respect to the former Minister for Mines, Jan Szlazak, I cannot agree with him when he states that coal and power are sold at market price.

Thus, provided that Endesa has some guarantee from Government that Opole's subsidy will continue, it is not surprising that they are eager to be involved.

There are some other interesting features about state of the art power stations.

## Jaworzno III

I visited Jan Kurp at this station in April 1999. He has a long-term contract to sell power at a good rate until 2008, 'because of my ecological activities' as he put it. Jaworzno has its own coal-mine. It is a joint enterprise, unique in the hard coal sector. The coal is high in sulphur, so Kurp has fitted both FGD and fluidised beds. His sulphur emissions are down by 80%. He is now 'EU compliant'.

Jaworzno backs up the assertion of Jean Trestour, former Chef D'Unite at DG Enlarge in Brussels, that a power station is 'a state within a state'. Jan Kurp's workforce has many welfare benefits, including recreation and, most importantly, a health centre. The National Health Service in Poland is not good and it is in practice necessary to pay for all treatment if one is to avoid a 12-month wait. Thus the Jaworzno Health Centre is a considerable encouragement for its employees.

It is in a way reminiscent of the old Communist system. Lord Haslam told me of two visits he made to a coal-mine before and after 1989. When the Communists were in charge they ran the mine with great expertise and many ancillary benefits, such as a health centre, and a 60 bed hospital. The miners were a privileged workforce. On Lord Haslam's return he found a well meaning Solidarity Worker in charge. He was 26 and 'did not know the first thing about mining'.

## Old and Dirty Power Stations

The Poles are less keen to show these to visitors, and the only one I have visited is Laziska, which has some dry FGD and is also a fine example of piecemeal modernisation. Parts of this station date from the 1920s.

\* \* \*

Generally, the whole manner in which the Polish power stations are developing is governed by the price they can charge for electricity; the contracts that they can secure or that Government can secure for them. A key player is the National Grid, or PSE. In theory it is no more than a humble carrier of power, in practice it is rather more than that.

# CHAPTER 9

## The National Grid (PSE) and the Sale of Electricity

Zmijewski is head of the grid. The nature of this network makes it probable that his aims will be different from those of the regulator, Juchniewicz, and indeed the two men have arguments over pricing. The grid suffers from a Communist legacy. Prices of electricity in the 60s and 70s were artificially low and resulted in excessive power use and hence a deficit in production capacity. This resulted in arbitrary disconnection of customers by dispatchers, depending upon their significance to the national economy.

Before the Second World War the largest power stations were industrial. There were no less than 3,000 public, private and municipally owned stations but they were very small. Annual power consumption amounted to only 300 Gwh.

It was the War that forced the power sector to centralise. The office of State Power Dispatch was created, and this determined the sequence of power supply to customers, according to national importance.

The present size of the entire transmission, distribution and supply system is as follows:

Transmission:

300 km of 750 kV line, from the Ukraine.
4,000 km of 400 kV line.
8,000 km of 220 kV line.

Distribution:

30,000 km of 110 kV line connected to more than 1,000 substations whence run:
260,000 km of 15 kV and 20 kV line.
360,000 km of 4 kV lines, connected to over 160,000 substations.

Supply:

The above substations connect with low voltage lines and also directly with industrial customers and the railways.

Thus there are four 'stages of electricity' with the price per unit rising at each. These are generation, transmission, distribution and supply.

In the mid 1990s the question of polluting the atmosphere became important.

'Environmental requirements create a specific investment market in Poland's power sector. Meeting the admissible $SO_2$ pollution levels due to apply at the beginning of 1998 will need investment of US$500 million. The investment programme needed to meet the requirements of the Second Sulphur Protocol will cost an additional US$1.3 billion by the year 2005.'

The document from which I quote is written by the Minister of Industry and Trade in March 1996 and is described as 'a paper adopted by the Council of Ministers in September 1996'.

It is a white paper listing intentions. The realities must await the Energy Law. This law was passed by both Houses in 1997, and it is fair to say that it does not consummate the hopes of the white paper.

111

I will quote three more sections from the 1996 paper, for they show that the Energy Law also aimed to achieve the following:

1. The Energy Regulatory Authority (i.e., Juchniewicz) will thoroughly supervise the wholesale tariff, the charges for transmission and the tariffs set by distribution companies to final customers.

2. The responsibility of the PSE for the continuity of supply to distributors is associated with the development of the National Power programme. Following the withdrawal of PSE from wholesale trading in the domestic market the scope of such works may be reduced and will mainly serve the purpose of planning the development of the transmission grid.

BUT

3. The efficient functioning of PSE is of key importance to the development of the electricity market with the maintenance of the National Power Security level and ensuing macro-economic and external conditions. *For these reasons the mediation of PSE in wholesale trading will be maintained for a period of 4 to 5 years.* (My emphasis.)

The famous Energy Law has now been on the statute book for three years.

It first established the Energy Regulatory Authority, with the regulator elected for a five-year period that cannot be terminated by the Government.

Secondly it established the principle of third-party access to the Grid. This unfortunately is limited to Polish based companies, so it does not help Poland's hopes of EU accession.

International third-party access is part of the *Acquis*. It gives foreign companies the right to sell electricity to each other via the Polish Grid, much as they can sell goods to each other via Polish road or rail. Poland hinders its own accession by denying foreign access to its grid.

The initial reaction to the Energy Law was that it was deficient in specific measures, and that 37 pieces of secondary legislation were needed to give the main law 'teeth'. I will discuss these in greater detail under the *Acquis* section.

Critics accuse the Poles of creating grandiose theories which permit them to avoid specifics. Thus the Energy Law separates energy into:
1. Creation
2. Regulation
3. Ownership.

When I met Juchniewicz in 1998 he merely said that he 'could not comment on measures that had not been passed by Government'.

On the other hand, when I visited the PSE in 1998 Marek Zerka, Director of Corporate Strategy told me that the prices of electricity would be decided by the regulator by January 1999. At that time Bicki was head of the Grid. Later in '98 he was removed, mainly because he was an SLD appointee. He was replaced by Zmijewski. This raises another problem with Polish non-Government appointments. They are all party political. We are fortunate in this country with Directors of the Regulatory Authority such as Littlechild and MacCarthy who are impartial. Also, the Polish regulator was not functioning in 1998.

A year later Juchniewicz the regulator was in place. I revisited the Grid and met Zmijewski in person to find him at daggers drawn with Juchniewicz. He accused Juchniewicz of reneging on the long-term contracts struck between the PSE and power stations between 1993 and 1997. He further stated that Juchniewicz had raised prices by 800% for some consumers.

Juchniewicz assured me that in no case had he raised prices by more than 13%, though a realist would raise them by 30%. Zmijewski was using installed capacity to arrive at his amazing figure of 800%. Juchniewicz said, reasonably 'Tariffs must reflect costs. These will be arrived at jointly by generators, distributors and the Grid'.

The long-term contract is probably the most important barrier to free trade in electricity.

70% of electricity is sold by such contracts and many of them stretch 12 years into the 21st century. They have all been agreed by generators and the Grid.

The contracts enable the bigger generators (e.g., Opole, Dolna Odra, Turow) to take out 10.5 billion zloty investment loans. The guaranteed high electricity contract selling price enables generators to repay the loans. They are needed to modernise equipment and clean up emissions and are laudable objectives.

Thus the Grid, though in theory nothing more than a beast of burden carrying current, was still fixing both the buying and selling price of electricity in 1999. This naturally caused friction with the regulator.

The Government aims to privatise the grid in 2001. The Government states it will; 'turn over its shares in the long-term power purchase agreements to the distribution companies (RECs)'. Since these contracts are such barriers to the free market I do not see distribution companies welcoming them.

When privatisation does happen:

'Generators will no longer be obliged to sell their output to the PSE. They will be able to sell into Pool Markets and/or agree contracts direct with Distribution companies, large consumers, or other market intermediaries such as trading companies. Similarly, rather than buying direct from PSE, distributors will be able to buy direct from the Pool or agree contracts with specific generators. PSE's role will change as it focuses solely on operating the grid rather than also managing the wholesale market for electricity. This role will be carried out by a new Electric Energy Exchange Company.'[1]

Then, according to the Central and Eastern European Business Information Centre (CEEBIC) net market research: 'The creation of an energy exchange was planned in 1996. Its final shape is still being discussed. The Polish Government is in the process of preparing a draft law on commodities exchange which will allow the establishment of the Energy Exchange (in Polish 'Gielda'). The law should be enacted in June 1999.'

I was fortunate enough to meet Juchniewicz for a third time, in summer 2000. This was a surprising meeting, to say the least. Most of the things which I thought would not happen had happened. Several of the forecasts listed above have been shown to be wrong: for instance the 1996 Government White Paper prediction that 'the Grid would mediate in wholesale trading for four or five years'. It now seems likely that the Grid will be privatised very soon and there are even fears that it will

1 Frank Harris, of Wood MacKenzie Consultants, Feb 4 1999.

go bankrupt. Juchniewicz now has many powers. He can approve all prices and will soon be able to set them. That is, prices for the Grid, the generators and the distribution companies.

He can also set 'justified costs' to cover environmental protection. He has already done so, causing electricity prices to rise faster than inflation. In 1999 inflation was 9.8% and electricity was up 12%. He assured me that Poland was now in line with Kyoto requirements and would continue to be so in 2020. He is involved in planning mergers between groups of both generators and RECs, and in their privatisation.

The largest REC is that of Upper Silesia and its sale should be completed by the end of 2000. The buyers are the same as those for Rybnik power station: that is, Marubeni, NRG and GE Capital.

Future planned sales are of the Warsaw REC to Swedish Vatenfall, followed by the Northern Group, known as G8, scheduled for the second quarter of 2001. In this group there are Gdansk, Torun, Elblag, Olsztyn, Koszalin and Slupsk in the north as well as Plock and Kalisz in central Poland.

In all cases only 20 to 25% of the shares will be put on the market. The Treasury will continue to be the majority shareholder. The privatisation is only partial. However it will eventually extend to all RECs. Following the G8 group the smallest south-eastern group will be privatised. This comprises Zeork, Rzeszow, Lublin, Lubzel and Zamosc. These in turn will be followed by the western group: Poznan, Bydgoszcz, Szczecin, Lodz, Teren and Opole. Then the southern group: Bedzin, Krakow, Biesko-Biala and Tarnow.

Juchniewicz's biggest problem remains the long-term power purchase agreement. He talked of turning a long-term agreement into a financial agreement, by compensating the power stations, though I cannot see how he proposes to fund this. The idea of 'turning the long-term power purchase agreements over to the RECs' which I mentioned previously seems to have disintegrated. This is not surprising as these agreements are liabilities. Juchniewicz next told me that the power purchase agreements covered 70% of the market and that the remaining 30% would be traded on the Energy Exchange.

I could not believe that the Energy Exchange (Gielda Energii SA) had come into being. But it had. The CEEBIC forecast of June 1999 for its creation was six months early. It actually came into being on Dec 9 1999 and started trading in summer 2000. The exchange is remarkable in that it is 20% foreign owned by Vattenfall and is actually structured in a more advanced manner than the UK Energy Exchange which took 18 years of Conservative rule to create.

I met Jacek Brandt, head of the Exchange. He told me that membership of this exchange was voluntary, which prima facie means that it can be bypassed. Nevertheless the Scandinavian system on which it is modelled is also voluntary, as are others in Amsterdam and Lisbon.

'The advantage of a voluntary system is that a zero bid can be bypassed' he told me.

Here in the UK we attempted to operate a compulsory exchange which turned out not to be a true exchange as it was only a sellers' market. Buyers were fairly impotent and traders were non-existent.

The Polish Exchange is expecting to attract 250 members, generators, traders, and RECs: in other words all the elements that make up a true market place. When I was in Warsaw the exchange was embarking on a series of computer training sessions with the new players: 24 at a time. Two of these are the two best power stations in Poland: Polaniec and Rybnik.

Thus the exchange has come into being at the same time as Juchniewicz has acquired considerable powers of price regulation himself. In theory Juchniewicz and his tariffs should be at loggerheads with the free market. This worries neither Juchniewicz nor Brandt. The worry remains the long-term power purchase agreement.

Juchniewicz's adviser is Dr Miroslaw Duda who works for Bechtel-US Aid Energy Group.

His solutions to the long-term contract problem are as follows:

1. Liquidate them.
2. Issue securities or bonds based on them.
3. Sell contracts to new trading companies.
4. Create a capacity reserve, funded as a part of the transmission service.

I do not understand Duda's solution number 4 and cannot see how Duda's solutions numbered 1 to 3 can possibly work. However, an article by Agnieska Berger in the newspaper *Puls Biznesu*, dated 26 January 2000 states that Zmijewski himself has said that thanks to compensatory fees the problem of the long-term contract between the Grid and power stations will be solved.

But no one could tell me where the money was coming from.

# CHAPTER 10

## The Polish Environment

'Poland uses 7.3 times as much energy per unit of GDP as does Western Europe' (a claim by the European Bank for Reconstruction and Development, EBRD).

The environment in Poland is not good: that includes the built environment. The blocks of flats in which most urban Poles live are jerry-built. They are poorly insulated against winter temperatures that plunge to minus 20. Therefore the Polish householder will use more heat and power than his Western counterpart.

The price charged to him will be less than the cost of production. Nevertheless it will be a higher percentage of his income than is the case in the West. One in three Polish householders will not pay his heat and power bills.

Against this background it would seem best to break the Polish environment into three sections:
1. The present state.
2. Measures to promote energy efficiency.
3. Measures to promote clean coal.

### 1. The Present State

Environmental issues can themselves be divided into three categories according to whether they are solid, liquid, or gaseous.

Solid environmental blight consists of eyesores such as industrial waste tips, slag and spoil heaps, and areas of devastation caused by open cast mining These include dead forests.

Liquid blight has already been mentioned in the salting up of the rivers by the washing of black coal. In addition there is virtually no treatment of sewage. Urban waste water treatment is high on the agenda. Drinking water standards also fall well short of those obtained in the West.

Both solid and liquid pollution is serious enough but they affect only Poles and are therefore less likely to prove a barrier to EU accession than gaseous pollution.

The main aerial pollutants are $SO_2$, Nox and dust. $CO_2$ is not toxic but does contribute to global warming: a separate issue to be addressed later.

Slocock, in his *Environmental Issues in EU Enlargement* gives quite an encouraging table. In the period 1985 to 1994:
$SO_2$ fell by 39%
Nox by 27%
Dust by 42%.

The quality of air in the cities improved by greater amounts. Over the same period:
$SO_2$ fell by 61%
Nox by 77 %
Dust by 54%.
(Source, Organisation for Economic Co-operation and Development.)
Slocock does stress the importance of relating these figures to GDP.
Bulgaria, for instance, has a poor environmental policy but has achieved greater reductions due to economic collapse.

Thus it is relevant to chart Poland's economic growth and energy supply from 1989 to 1994.

| Year | 1989 | 1990 | 1991 | 1992 | 1993 | 1994 |
|---|---|---|---|---|---|---|
| GDP growth in % | 0.2 | -11.6 | -7.0 | 2.6 | 3.8 | 9.2 |
| Primary Energy Supply | -3.7 | -16.3 | -4.3 | -6.1 | 1.9 | -0.8 |

(GDP growth from World Bank 1997, Table 1.1, *Energy from British Petroleum 1997*, p37.)

These make Slocock's $SO_2$ and Nox reductions less significant but still important.

It is undoubtedly true that the greatest improvements to Poland's environment would be effected by myriad changes on the demand side. These however are hard to enforce and even harder to measure.

Elizabeth Favrat has measured the specific actions undertaken by the supply side.

Her doctoral thesis for Sussex University is on Polish energy. Her tables show the environmental measures taken in some power and CHP Stations. Interestingly her tables show that the major partners in the clean up are foreign. This goes some way to explain why the West is investing in the most expensive power: not the cheapest, as suggested by Juchniewicz. The reason is that it is all part of a package. The West installs equipment and then negotiates a long-term contract for expensive electricity from the newly modernised power station. The down side remains: who pays for the long-term contract?

**FAVRAT TABLES I**

| Power Plant | Project | Capacity | Major Partners* | Stage |
|---|---|---|---|---|
| Belchatow PP | Flue gas desulphurisation | 2(+2)x360 | Netherlands, Kema, SEP, Hoogovens ETS, NFEP | E |
| Bielsko-Biala CHP | Finalisation of feasibility study, strategy of privatisation, Grid's financing of CHP modernisation, and equipment with fluidised bed boiler | 1x135 | EBRD, Austria, Credit-anstalt BkVerein, PPGC | E |
| Dolna-Odra PP | Two electrostatic precipitators | 2x200 | Denmark, Danish Firm | C |
| Dolna-Odra PP | Low-NOx burners | 2x200 | Denmark, Danish firm | E |
| *Dolna-Odra PP* | *Feasibility study for desulphurisation system and modernisation under a Joint Venture* | *2x200* | *EBRD, potentially EdF, Vattenfall, Preussenelektra, ABB* | *P* |
| Elblag CHP | Flue gas desulphurisation, refurbishment | 1x260 | Sweden, Swedish firm | P |
| Jaworzno III PP | Flue gas desulphurisation | 2x200 | KEMA, Polish firm, German firm | E |
| Jaworzno III PP | Installation of Low-NOx burners | 2x200 | Finland, IVO, Tampella (FL) | E |
| Kozienice PP | Flue gas desulphurisation | n.a. | Japan Int. Cooperation Agency | C |
| *Krakow Leg CHP* | *Privatisation and modernisation of CHP plant* | *n.a.* | *World Bank, EdF, National Power, Vattenfall* | *S* |
| Lagisza PP | Modernisation with low-NOx burners | n.a. | Netherlands, Rafako, Stork Ketels BV | C |

cont.

| Power Plant | Project | Capacity | Major Partners* | Stage |
|---|---|---|---|---|
| *Lagisza PP* | *Desulphurisation, refurbishment, asb and waste management* | *n.a.* | *Rafako?, International bidding announced* | *n.a.* |
| Opole PP | Flue gas desulphurisation | 3x360 | KEMA (NL), German firm | E |
| *Patnow II PP* | *Refurbishment of two Boilers under a Joint Venture and desulphurisation* | *2x200* | *EBRD?, Vattenfall, IVO, ABB Flakt* | *S* |
| *Pruszkow 2 CHP* | *Erection of a CHP unit (125MW) with FGD* | *1x125* | *PPGC, Warsaw CHP company, possible bidding* | *P* |
| Siekerki CHP | Low-NOx burners | n.a. | Rafako, Stork | E |
| *Sierza PP* | *Desulphurisation units* | *2x125(4x?)* | *Kloeckner SHL (G), Elektrim* | *n.a.* |
| *Sierza PP* | *Fluidised bed combustion, rehabilitation of turbine-sets* | *2x130* | *CdF(F)* | *n.a.* |
| Skawina PP | Technical assistance and construction of FGD in power plant (wet process) | 2x | USA, Airpol (US), Rafako, Ecofund, NFEP | E/C |
| Turow PP | Flue gas desulphurisation (dry) | 2x200 | ABB Flakt technology, Ecofund | C |
| Turow PP | Installation of fluidised bed combustion and rehabilitation of turbine sets | 2x200 | ABB, Steinmuller, Ahlstrom Pyropower, NFEP, Elektrim | E |
| *Wroclaw CHP* | *Semi-dry desulphurisation in CHP* | *n.a.* | *EdF, Elektrim* | *n.a.* |
| *Zeran CHP* | *Fluidised bed boilers* | *2x100* | *USA?, Rafako* | *n.a.* |

*Non-exhaustive

The data contained in this table cannot be cleared of uncertainties. The number of boiler units is sometimes an estimation. The projects in roman are the projects executed or under execution; projects in italics are still under negotiation. C, E, P and S respectively stand for: project completed under execution, proposal and stalled.

**FAVRAT TABLES II: Projects and least cost planning.**

| Project | Power Plant control | SO₂ Priorities* | Refurbishment |
|---|---|---|---|
| Flue gas desulphurisation | Belchatow PP | Wet scrubbers (4) | 3 |
| Feasibility study strategy of privatisation, Grid's financing of CHP modernisation, and equipment with fluidised bed boiler | Bielsko-Biala CHP | n.a. | n.a. |
| Two electrostatic precipitators | Dolna-Odra PP | Dry FGD (8) | 4 |
| Low-NOx burners | Dolna-Odra PP | " | " |
| *Feasibility study for desulphurisation system and modernistaon under a Joint Venture* | *Dolna-Odra PP* | " | " |
| *Flue gas desulphurisation, refurbishment* | *Elblag CHP* | *n.a.* | *n.a.* |
| Flue gas desulphurisation | Jaworzno III PP | Wet Scrubbers (4), Dry FGD (2) | 4 |
| Installation of Low-NOx burners | Jaworzno III PP | " | " |
| Flue gas desulphurisation | Kozienice PP | | 2 |
| *Privatisation and modernisation of CHP plant* | *Krakow Leg CHP* | | 2 |
| Modernisation with low-NOx burners | Lagisza PP | | 2 |
| *Desulphurisation, refurbishment asb and waste management* | *Lagisza PP* | 2 | |

cont.

| Project | Power Plant | SO$_2$ control | Refurbishment Priorities* |
|---|---|---|---|
| Flue gas desulphurisation | Opole PP | | |
| Refurbishment of two Boilers under a Joint Venture, and desulphurisation equipment | Patnow II PP | | Repowering |
| Erection of a CHP unit (125MW) with FGD | Pruszkow 2 CHP | | |
| Low-NOx burners | Sierkerki CHP | | |
| Desulphurisation units | Sierza PP | Dry FGD (6) | 2 |
| Fluidised bed combustion, rehabilitation of turbine-sets | Sierza PP | " | " |
| Technical assistance and construciton of FGD in power plant (wet process) | Skawina | | 1 (4 to be decommissioned |
| Flue gas desulphurisation (dry) | Turow PP | Dry FGD (3) | 6 units repowering. 1 decomm., option 3 for (8-10) |
| Installation of fluidised bed combustion and rehabilitation of turbine sets | Turow PP | " | " |
| Semi-dry desulphurisation in CHP | Wroclaw CHP | | |
| Fluidised bed boilers | Zeran CHP | | |

In SO$_2$ control, numbers in brackets indicate the number of boiler units to be retrofitted. The refurbishment priorities correspond to LCI recommendations (ABCD): 1 = doing nothing; 2 = life extension of 20 years; 3 = rehabilitaiton + additional improvements; 4 = 3 + further life extension. Source: Own elaboration and *Least Cost Investment Study for the Polish Power Sector* (1994)

The above tables show considerable improvements but should not conceal the main picture.

Poland is well behind the West in her air quality. It will cost billions of dollars for her to catch up.

## $CO_2$ and Global Warming

This issue is separate from the preventive measures described above, as they are dealing with poisonous gases. $CO_2$ is not poisonous, but is a major contributor to climate change. What is more, climate change was not an issue when many of the above systems to reduce $SO_2$ and Nox were installed. Some of them actually increase the emissions of carbon dioxide.

However Poland's commitment not to exceed 1988 levels of $CO_2$ emissions has been met.

By 1995 they were down by 20 to 25%.

Two factors may reverse this downward trend:

1. The increasing amount of coal generated electricity exported to the West.

2. The increase in road transport. The number of private cars doubles every five years.

Poland has another commitment, which is to reduce greenhouse gases to 82% of their 1988 level by 2010. This will be harder to achieve given the policy stated in the *National Report of Poland* (1995) that 'greenhouse gas reduction is not a priority goal given our pressing social and economic problems'. A country study undertaken with support from the US Government concludes that Poland will meet her 2010 target, but thereafter, 'only those scenarios which include the nuclear option or assume a very optimistic ability of the Polish economy will result in reductions'.

## 2. Measures to Promote Energy Efficiency

There are several organisations attempting to do this but generally they suffer from lack of funding.

KAPE (in English, The Polish National Conservation Industry) is attempting to raise public awareness and to provide training programmes for energy conservation in the 50 to 100 KW range. It is run by Marina Coey.

EKOFUND is co-financing 24 coal to gas conversion projects with assistance from the Norwegians.

The then EC set up 13 Energy Centres between 1991 and 1996. However they were only funded for the initial few years. None of them achieved financial self-sufficiency and most have now closed.

The USA set up 5 Energy Efficiency centres. The centre in Poland is called FEWE and is run by Adam Gula.

There are larger European organisations that I will consider under the *Acquis* section of the book. There is a Climate Technology Institute, SCORE and Energy Service companies, called ESCOs.

Purely Polish organisations also include:

Energie Cites, Poland's Ecofund, and the Fund for Environmental Protection.

Poland does have a tax levied on $CO_2$ emissions. The charge only has symbolic meaning since it is so low. However the fact that it already exists might make it easier to raise its level.

Poland should meet its international commitments regarding $CO_2$ emissions but it does not pursue an active policy specifically aimed at greenhouse gas abatement. It is among the top 15 global $CO_2$ emitters (Russia is third, the Ukraine seventh and Poland twelfth).

## 3. Clean Coal Technologies

The World Coal Institute maintains that the concept of coal as a dirty fuel is a Victorian legacy. It claims that modern coal is as clean as any other fuel and we should look elsewhere for the causes of deforestation and acid rain which are commonly attributed to the gases resulting from coal burning. This is special pleading. However there are a number of technologies that make coal less dirty and I would like to list these in this chapter. The emissions to be tackled are of particulates, of the toxic gases $SO_2$ and Nox, and of the greenhouse gas carbon dioxide.

Particulates are the most visible emissions. It is these that caused the great smogs of London familiar to readers of Sherlock Holmes, and caused in particular a smog in 1954 that killed thousands and resulted in the UK's Clean Air Act of 1957. Particulate removal is widespread in Poland and can be implemented in a number of ways.

*Particulates* (or soot) are impurities in the coal and can be partially removed by *dense media separation*. The coal is floated across a tank of suitable liquid and floats whilst the particulates fall to the bottom.

*Pulverised fuel combustion* enables most particulates to be removed from the flue gases after burning. These gases pass horizontally between the collecting plates of an electrostatic precipitator. An electric field creates a charge on the particulates which are then drawn towards the plates. Periodically, the plates vibrate and shake the dust into a hopper.

*Fabric filters* do much the same job. They are similar to huge vacuum cleaner bags.

*Nitrous oxide* is reduced by burning coal at low temperatures with a paucity of oxygen.

*Sulphur dioxide* is a damaging substance as it forms sulphuric acid when combined with water and forms acid rain. It corrodes buildings and pollutes waterways. It is probably the main cause of forest death. Much sulphur can be removed from coal by washing it, but the main means of removing it is by flue gas desulphurisation. The sulphur passes through a sorbent of limestone and water and forms gypsum, a useful building material. The disadvantage of FGD is its cost and size. It is in effect a huge chemical plant bolted on to a power station. It is bigger than the power station. There are handling problems in transporting the limestone to the power station and taking the gypsum away.

Typical Coal-Fired Power Station with Flue Gas Desulphurisation

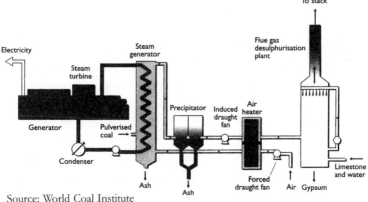

Source: World Coal Institute

The efficiency of burning all fuels is increased considerably with moves to high temperature and high-pressure steam conditions. *Sub critical* (<221.2 bar) achieves efficiency of 36 to 38%. *Supercritical* (>221.2 bar) achieves over 45%. There are plants operating in Denmark, Japan and Opole in Poland. Development of new steels now allows steam conditions to be raised to *Ultra-supercritical.* Here pressures are greater than 246 bar and temperatures in excess of 566 degrees centigrade. Ultra-supercritical is still at the experimental stage. Only Denmark, Germany and Japan have pilot projects.

## Fluidised Beds

Fluidised beds are popular with European governments of all political persuasions when arguing the case for clean coal. They are seen as a panacea to all noxious emissions and to global warming. The latter may be true to an extent as all fluidised beds burn more efficiently and therefore emit less $CO_2$.

Fluidised beds were invented by Winkler in 1922. In the Second World War they were used to manufacture synthetic petrol, for oil cracking, and for the roasting of metallic ores. They were then found to be efficient burners of poor quality fuels such as wood pulp, anthracite culm and poor quality coal, high in sulphur. There are three types.

In the *simple fluidised bed* coal is burnt in a bed of ash and limestone. Air is blown upwards into this bed. It behaves like a boiling liquid. It is said to be fluidised. Water pipes are immersed in the bed and the steam from them drives a conventional turbine.

In the *circulating fluidised bed* high velocity gases circulate unburnt solids: ash, limestone and coal to cyclones where they are separated from the gases and recycled to the combustion chamber.

In the *pressurised fluidised bed* the air is delivered to the bed at 12 to 16 bar. Crushed coal and limestone, possibly mixed with water, forms a pumpable paste. The temperature is around 850 degrees Centigrade. Again, the unburnt solids are removed by cyclones and returned to the combustion chamber. The main advantage of the pressurised bed is that the flue gases are at sufficient temperature to drive a gas turbine. At the same time water pipes immersed in the bed drive a steam turbine. The two turbines are complementary. Steam turbines work at low temperatures and high pressures: gas turbines at high temperatures and low pressures.

Efficiency from a PFB is reckoned at over 46%. But fluidised beds of all types need double the quantity of limestone to absorb the sulphur as does normal FGD.

Pressurised Fluidised Bed Combined Cycle

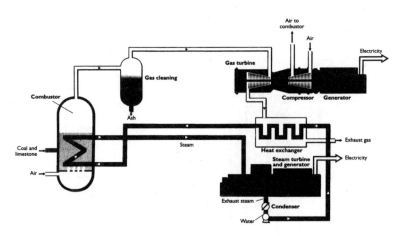

Source: World Coal Institute

Pressurised fluidised bed combustion is described as a direct system. An indirect system is:

## The Integrated Gasification Combined Cycle (IGCC)

This involves the indirect combustion of a fuel gas in the turbine. Coal is brought into contact with oxygen and steam. Partial combustion takes place to produce a fuel gas, comprising mainly carbon monoxide and hydrogen which powers a gas turbine. Waste heat from the fuel gas is then used to produce steam to drive a steam turbine. Whilst these plants are still in the commercial demonstration stage, efficiencies are expected to rise to 50% in the future.

IGCC systems produce less Nox, Sox and $CO_2$. Up to 99% of the sulphur present in the coal can be recovered for sale as chemically pure sulphur. There is a prototype IGCC station at Buggenum in the Netherlands of 250 MWe.

Integrated Coal Gasification Combined Cycle Unit

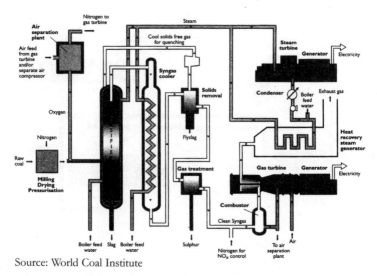

Source: World Coal Institute

There is also conventional gasification of coal – the old 'towns' gas: a widespread practice in Europe before the arrival of natural gas. All gasification will produce pollutants, so there is a seductive technique to gasify coal underground; that is, in situ at the pit face. Gases are never released to the atmosphere. But the technique, tried in Spain, is extraordinarily dangerous with risks of both fire and explosion.

All clean coal technologies add cost to the power produced. This is significant for Poland who is in any event having difficulty in bringing its power costs down.

Ian Torrens of Shell gives the types of technology examined in 1995 by emerging countries:
Sub Critical Pulverised Fuel Combustion: safe and cheap.
Supercritical: technically possible but more costly and risky.
IGCC: too expensive.

He forecasts that in 2005 the following technologies will be installed:
1. Supercritical steam.
2. Pressurised fluidised beds, but only in 'niche' markets.
3. IGCC in pilot plants.

Jim Watson, in his thesis for Sussex University, compares two technologies: that of the fluidised bed for coal and that of the combined cycle gas turbine for natural gas. He describes fluidised beds as 'a short lived niche market' and the gas turbine in contrast as a major success. He attributes this to the falling price of natural gas worldwide.

But Poland is at present so dependent on coal that this choice is not available to her. She must decide which is the better clean coal technology: flue gas desulphurisation units or fluidised beds.

Fluidised beds are more expensive than 'bolt on' flue gas desulphurisation units: that is, the retention of the existing boiler and turbine and a simple addition of FGD as an end of pipe technology. However this is not comparing like with like. A better comparison would be a fluidised bed and a completely new unit incorporating FGD: new boiler, new turbine, new desulphurisation unit. In the opinion of the construction company Energoprojekt of Katowice, the fluidised bed is actually cheaper in this case by 10 to 15%. Furthermore they are efficient systems emitting less $CO_2$ than do FGD/Low Nox systems. The latter emit more $CO_2$, as more coal must be burnt to power them.

Energoprojekt is wholly owned by its employees. It has built 311 boilers and 148 turbine sets, adding up to 10,200 MW, which is a third of Poland's capacity.

This company has no vested interest in promoting fluidised beds so their judgement is surely trustworthy. They claim also that Polish $SO_2$ emissions are now less than those of EU countries. In 1990 $SO_2$ represented 50% of total emissions but this had reduced to 30% by 1999. If this is the case they are complying with the Large Combustion Plant Directive.

Brussels is of the opinion that they are not. They cannot both be right.

It is surely right that the best way for Poland to clean up her environment is by abandoning coal altogether and switching to gas or nuclear. Indeed the Commission's opinion on Poland's application for membership is, 'that coal will be increasingly substituted by imports of natural gas' (15/7/97).

There is no such thing as clean coal technology, only cleaner coal technology.

# CHAPTER 11

## Polish and United Kingdom's Energy Compared

Vicente Luque Cabal is the coal expert at the Commission's Energy Directorate. He gave me an interesting chart showing that the Polish coal industry of the mid 1990s was similar to the UK industry of the mid 1970s.

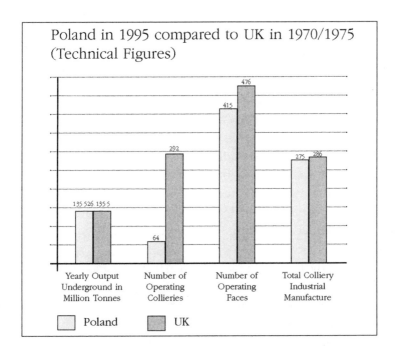

Poland in 1995 compared to UK in 1970/1975 (Technical Figures)

| | Yearly Output Underground in Million Tonnes | Number of Operating Collieries | Number of Operating Faces | Total Colliery Industrial Manufacture |
|---|---|---|---|---|
| Poland | 135.526 | 64 | 415 | 275 |
| UK | 135.5 | 292 | 476 | 286 |

There is a tendency for all Governments to subsidise a polluting fuel when logically they should be taxing it. The United Kingdom is no exception to this trend. Indeed I will argue that its record is rather worse than Poland's.

In the First World War the UK had around one million miners working in thousands of small privately owned pits. But it had also an Empire on which the sun never set and this gave it access to oil. Even in 1916, Beatty's Battlecruisers at Jutland were oil fired. The Middle East was a British fiefdom. The Suez Canal a British waterway. We owned half of Shell and created the Anglo Iranian Oil Company, later renamed BP.

Using hindsight, it seems peculiar that the miners wielded such power when our access to cheap oil was unlimited. Yet until 1974 the miners were strong enough to black out the country and to bring down the Government.

After the Second World War the United Kingdom possessed the atomic bomb, and from this stemmed the birth of 'Atoms for Peace' and a nuclear power sector. In those days all nuclear news was good news. There was even a device called Zeta, reputed to produce limitless energy from nothing. Today's equivalent could be cold fusion. Whilst there were many pipe dreams there was also a steady build of magnox power stations followed by Advanced Gas Cooled Reactors. These would provide around one fifth of our electricity.

At the same time however Mossadeq had the temerity to claim that Iranian oil was, in fact, Iranian. The loss of control of the Middle East was worrying for BP in particular. Before I become too critical of Poland's fear of reliance on Russian gas it is wise to remember the fears in this country over an independent Middle East, and how we even went to war over Suez in 1956.

Within BP it made sense to diversify supplies: Alaska and then the North Sea. These became yet more important as the price of oil soared after the Yom Kippur War.

Another important North Sea product was natural gas. As we converted our cookers and fires to this cleaner fuel the noxious gas works serving each community disappeared. Coal/gas conversion was a thing of the past. More importantly, it became an attractive option to generate electricity from natural gas fired power stations.

British coal fired power stations were normally built on top of the coalfields. The coastal power stations imported coal at world price and this became the cheapest fuel.

Orimulsion was yet another alternative to British coal.

Against this background it is remarkable that the British coal industry remained so powerful. According to Winskel's 1985 thesis on the privatisation of the Electrical Supply Industry (ESI):

'From the mid 1950s onwards the dominance of the coal fired steam turbine in the British ESI was in part a reflection of the political management of the energy industries, as the ESI was used by successive governments to provide a protected market for the British coal industry.'

Thus, when the miners struck in 1974 it seemed reasonable for Heath to declare a National State of Emergency. This included staggered working hours, no office heating, and no television after 10 p.m.

The change came with the Conservative victory of 1979 and a Prime Minister so robust that when faced with another strike in 1984 she instructed the Head of the Central Electricity Generating Board, Walter Marshall to 'keep the lights on whatever the cost'. The eventual collapse of this strike was brought about by the divide and conquer principle. Those miners working in Nottinghamshire were guaranteed their jobs and a very healthy pay packet. They continued to produce coal. Since British Rail would not carry it, it was transported by road. This was, incidentally, found to be cheaper than rail in any event.

As the National Union of Mineworkers (NUM) President Arthur Scargill saw that the electrical industry could keep going without power cuts indefinitely the strike finally collapsed. Then we saw on our television screens the tragic sight of miners marching back to work headed by their brass bands when there was precious little work to go back to.

As the Thatcher Government progressed so it furthered its goals of a free and competitive market for energy. This would be achieved by privatisation of the generating board, the Grid, the regional electricity companies and the mines. These goals are similar to those at which Poland is presently aiming.

Strangely this brought the British Government up against the same problems that the Polish Government is facing as it converts to a market economy. Some elements of the energy sector had never been costed. The main surprise was the expense of generating nuclear electricity. The original split of the Central Electricity Generating Board (CEGB) into 70% National Power and 30% Powergen, was biased towards National Power as it was to include the nuclear sector. But the City was simply not interested in nuclear so we soon had the peculiar hybrid of privatised fossil fuel generation but state owned nuclear generation.

However, British deep mined coal was also expensive so pits had to close. The Westminster debates on that were interesting.

The then opposition stressed the destruction of entire communities. They brought to mind the unemployment of the 1930s, now returning, and of the Jarrow March.

Meanwhile a South African miner asked me if our Government was subsidising a museum for the benefit of old coal miners and Michael Heseltine remarked, 'I have been given the job of selling 40 million tonnes of British coal and I cannot find a market for it.'

Thus it has come to be that the 1984 defeat of the miners was by no means complete and that we are still subsidising a polluting industry producing 30 million tonnes a year of rather expensive coal.

In early 2000 the Government gave Richard J. Budge, the head of our largest coal mining company, RJB Mining, a grant of £100 million. The private sector, meanwhile, has recognised that the most profitable means of electricity generation is by combined cycle gas turbine and as we mark time on coal and stop building new nuclear stations the 'Dash for Gas' is proceeding apace.

Natural gas emits less $SO_2$ and $CO_2$ than coal. This puts the present Government in a fix, for we are signatories to Rio, Kyoto, and various sulphur protocols. Government is green, yet it is traditionally the miners' best friend.

This dilemma is highlighted by an extract from the Department of Trade and Industry (DTI) consultation document 'Review of Energy Sources for Power Generation' of 25 June 1998:

'There have been calls on Government…to actually guarantee a specific share of the electricity market for UK deep mined coal. The Government does not believe that to identify a defined share of the market regardless of other considerations is the right course to take. Its aim is to put all fuels on a level playing field, and not to give priority to any one. The Government does not propose to subsidise any part of the UK coal industry. Coal producers themselves have asked for fairness, not favours.'

But since elected in 1997 Government has been back-pedalling on the building of yet more CCGT stations. They initiated an energy review resulting in a five-year moratorium.

The Review prompted the following from David Lewis of Enron in January 1999 at a Centrepoint, London, seminar:

'The results of the Government's Energy Review have damaged the prospects for the use of gas in power generation for a period likely to be at least five years and in doing so will damage the UK economy and environment. However, the Government cannot continue to ration new power station consents if it wishes to promote environmental improvements and to allow the UK economy to succeed. Provided the moratorium is lifted then in the longer term the amount of gas used in power generation is likely to return to the levels which would have occurred without the current intervention in the market…There will be a second 'Dash for Gas.'

The Government also finds it important to maintain a diversity of supply. It claims that coal fired stations are uniquely good at providing peak supplies: at coping with sudden surges caused by cold weather or the end of a popular television programme. This capability is called 'load following'.

Actually, this Government claim is wrong. CCGT stations could load follow equally well if they were adapted to do so. It is the nuclear stations that cannot do this.

The best argument against gas comes from the DTI green paper of 25 June 1998:

'On the evidence produced by our independent gas consultants we could be importing about one third of our gas supplies by 2010 and 55 to 90% by 2020. Although the European Gas Market, on which we will become increasingly dependent, is well supplied and increasingly flexible, it too will be moving towards significant dependence on imports, reaching a level of 75% of consumption by 2020, as the consultants noted' (paragraph 23).

And at paragraph 24: 'That gas is likely to come from more remote sources with longer and more complicated transit routes. Although there is no major security problem in prospect at present, there is clearly a range of political and other uncertainties and a need to consider the risk of disruption.'

Dependence on gas coming perhaps from Kazakhstan would put us in the same position as the Poles are at present.

## How We Trade Electricity

Before privatisation the Central Electricity Generating Board could dictate the price that the Regional Electricity Companies paid for power. It operated a merit order, whereby the cheapest power stations were chosen as first, or base load, suppliers, and the most expensive were only called upon as a last resort. The CEGB could claim that their monopoly was not total, as England and Wales were also importing electricity from Scotland and France.

With privatisation the Government decided to continue this process with 'The Pool'. This was the spot market in electricity, determined at 10 a.m. each day for half-hour tranches the following day. Thus it is also a merit order in theory, but in theory only. For as we realised that nuclear power was expensive, we also realised that nuclear power could not be switched on at half an hour's notice. Nuclear therefore had to be base load, occupying the same niche as lignite does in Poland. The Polish position is the more logical of the two, for they use their cheapest stations the most frequently whereas we use our most expensive ones.

All power providers are paid at the System Marginal Price for each half-hour. That is, the price charged by the most expensive power station, plus a spare capacity charge, plus an uplift charge. Expensive base load stations will probably bid zero for all periods, as they cannot risk shutting down, particularly if they are nuclear. They gamble on a high spot price. The spot price can be raised artificially since there are comparatively few generating companies. It is tempting to declare a mid merit order power station as not working as this results in using a peak load station and of course all stations are then paid at the peak load price.

The unpredictable nature of the spot market makes it unattractive for major energy users, so all the RECs buy 90% of their supply by longer term bilateral trading, which is known as Contracts for Difference. Within this so called free market, which is in practice a supply market, not a demand one, and therefore not wholly free, operated the regulator. Stephen Littlechild, who retired in early 1999. He was unhappy with both the Pool and Contracts for Difference and has recommended a bilateral trading system likely to be adopted by Government. His successor, Callum MacCarthy, should implement this. MacCarthy also regulates gas. The two energy sources are now regarded as so similar that the Office of Electricity Regulator (OFFER) and the Office of Gas Regulator (OFFGAS) have joined to form the Office of Regulator (OFFREG). MacCarthy looks forward to 'An orderly market free of manipulation' (Institute of Energy seminar, 18 March 1999).

The Littlechild solution to energy trading has much in common with the system existing in Scandinavia.

The Poles have chosen to trade electricity using a system much freer than our own and, like that of Scandinavia, voluntary.

By March 1999 we had reduced the power of our few energy generators. At the Institute of Energy conference on 18 March, John Battle said:

'I do feel that most people in the UK are not aware of what I call the changing shape of the energy markets. There are now 30 major electricity generators, 20 electricity suppliers, 60 gas suppliers to the industrial market, and 27 gas suppliers to the domestic market... 'Multi Utilities' are also beginning to emerge, offering a range of services. All the public electricity suppliers offer gas across the market and gas companies are beginning to offer electricity. Water companies have merged with electricity utilities. The National Grid and Scottish Power have developed telecoms services which they have since sold.'

Deep mined British coal is expensive and dirty. It is British however and its reserves are immense. So for reasons both patriotic and political it still is the main fuel used in electrical generation.

From Michelle Aveline et al, *Generation in the 90s*, Oxford Economic Research Assistants I offer this table:

## Share of total electricity generated by type of plant 1996-2003

|  | 1996/97 | 2002/2003 |
| --- | --- | --- |
| Coal Fired Steam generation | 42% | 23% |
| CCGT | 28% | 56% |
| Nuclear | 28% | 20% |
| Oil | 2% | 1% |

# CHAPTER 12

## Polish and German Energy Compared

Vicente Luque Cabal also gave me a chart showing that the Polish coal industry of the mid 90s was similar to that of Germany in 1970.

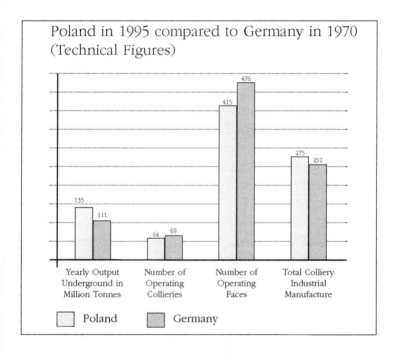

Poland in 1995 compared to Germany in 1970
(Technical Figures)

| | Yearly Output Underground in Million Tonnes | Number of Operating Collieries | Number of Operating Faces | Total Colliery Industrial Manufacture |
|---|---|---|---|---|
| Poland | 135 | 64 | 415 | 275 |
| Germany | 111 | 69 | 476 | 252 |

The German electricity energy market is large. Its capacity is 114 GW, compared to Poland's 30 GW and the UK's 55 GW. Germany is the world's third largest emitter of carbon dioxide. Only the USA and Japan are ahead of it. It also produces and consumes more black coal than any other country in Europe and more lignite than any other country in the world.

Germany forms the bridge between Western free markets and Eastern command markets. Three quarters of the country have developed in the Western tradition, but the other quarter, formerly the DDR, has a Communist tradition. Germany also has a considerable nuclear facility.

In 1991 the Government reassessed its energy objectives following re-unification and outlined the following broad goals:

1. Integration of the five new East German Länder into a market oriented energy supply system.

2. Reduction of $CO_2$ emissions in energy production as a first step towards a comprehensive climate change strategy.

3. Continued contribution of coal to the national energy supply, but under changed policy conditions.

4. A sustained role for nuclear power in the nation's energy mix.

5. Further international co-operation in the energy arena and expansion of the European Internal Market for Energy.

However, the Government, elected in September 1998, is Schröder's SPD Party (the German Social Democratic Party) allied to the Greens. They do not have the same broad goals, particularly regarding the promotion of hard coal and nuclear power. Indicative of the complexity of Germany's position is that both the most polluting and the least polluting fuels, black coal and renewable sources, are now subsidised.

In 1997 the Energy Law put a progressively reduced ceiling on hard coal subsidies for the period 1998 to 2005. The subsidies have been made more transparent, so that it is now possible to calculate that German coal costs three times as much to produce as does imported coal.

In 1994 the Electricity Feed Law obliged electricity companies to buy renewables at a premium. In the case of wind power the premium was 90% of the selling price to the consumer and this disadvantaged those fossil fuel companies generating in the North, for most wind farms are located on the Baltic Coast.

Germany has two thousand megawatts of wind power. She has more installed capacity than any other country, with the USA second, Denmark third and India fourth. It has 45% of the installed wind capacity of the EU. But together with other renewable resources, that is, biomass, hydropower and solar power these impressive looking percentages only provide for 1% of Germany's energy needs.

The Government puts large emphasis on energy efficiency. Major efforts have been made in the new Länder. Better insulation of buildings, the requirement to install heat consumption meters in dwellings, and an overall effort to reduce energy intensity go some way to reducing emissions.

Through this strategy the Government is hoping to reduce $CO_2$ emissions from the energy sector by 25 to 30% by 2005. This is an ambitious target, especially given the fact that the International Energy Agency is forecasting a rise over the next decade based on current policies and consumption patterns.

As the West German Government took over the East they achieved a considerable reduction in all emissions by either closing or retrofitting with flue gas desulphurisation (FGD) the lignite power stations. East Germany's lignite production has been reduced by two thirds. Furthermore there was a massive decrease in consumption in the new Länder. Total energy supply in the whole of Germany reduced by 8.1%

between 1988 and 1994. Thus in the early 1990s the figures were looking good but it has not been possible for Germany to continue reducing pollutants at the same rate after the fillip of closing dirty Eastern power stations ended. In 1996 total energy supply rose again, by 3.1%.

On 1 April 1999 the Schröder Government introduced an eco tax which was meant to create market incentives to switch to green power. Its effect will be to raise all energy prices by about 10% over the next three years. Strangely, renewable energy sold into the grid is not exempt from the tax, though the revenue generated will be used to fund renewable energy programmes.

It would be fair to say that Germany has just about every energy problem in the book: 5 poor Länder grafted onto the country; controversial nuclear power, a large deep mined coal industry and now a Government who cannot even subscribe to the broad objectives agreed ten years ago.

Germany's energy industry may be complex, but it is also the largest in Europe and important so I will look at it piecemeal.

### Energy Conservation and Efficiency Policy

The *Small Scale Production Plant Ordinance* sets maximum heat losses and pollution levels for combustion facilities with heat output of less than 1 MW for solid fuels or 5 MW for liquid fuels. Heat losses in existing plants must be progressively reduced to these levels.

The *Ordinance on Thermal Insulation* tightens regulations for new buildings and older buildings if substantially renovated. This is expected to reduce heating requirements by 30%.

There are fee based incentives for architects and engineers to offer more services related to energy saving.

## Natural Gas

Germany is the largest natural gas market in Europe. Total natural gas supply was 73.5 million tonnes of oil equivalent (Mtoe) in 1996. There are 330,000 kilometres of pipeline. Yet gas's contribution to electrical power generation is quite small.

In 1997 public power plant generation was fuelled as follows:

| | |
|---|---|
| Nuclear | 35% |
| Lignite | 28% |
| Hard coal | 26% |
| Natural Gas | 6% |
| Oil | 2% |
| Renewables | 1%   (IEA) |

The above list is skewed in favour of nuclear and lignite as these provide the base load. But it would ease Germany's task of Kyoto compliance if more combined cycle gas turbine stations were to replace those fired by hard coal. The gas is used for heating. It is replacing lignite as the main fuel for district heating schemes, particularly in the new Länder.

Only 22% of the gas is German, and that is of low calorific value. Germany imports the remainder mainly from Russia but also from Norway and the Netherlands. The largest company is Ruhrgas. It is owned by consortia belonging to the coal industry, steel mills and utilities as well as national and international oil companies. Ruhrgas itself owns Ruhrgasindustrie, which is involved in gas measurement and control, industrial furnaces, co-generation systems and engineering stations. It has shares in distribution companies and municipal gas companies in Hungary and Estonia.

Years of Ruhrgas's monopolistic control of Germany's gas market have left Germany with a highly developed gas infrastructure. Ruhrgas is now involved in laying pipes to connect Poland to the German system in order to increase imports of Russian gas via Poland. This project should be completed in 2001. Ruhrgas has also bought shares in Russia's Gazprom in an effort to better relations between the two companies. This anticipates future increases in the German demand for gas.

Competition in the market has developed slowly. Ruhrgas's main competitor, Wingas, was formed in 1990. By the end of 1997 Wingas had become Germany's sixth largest company.

Wingas is now gaining market share, whilst Ruhrgas is losing it. It is Wingas that is building the pipeline that will connect Russia's Yamal peninsula to the German network. With these two big companies competing there is now a retail gas market which allows consumers a choice among both suppliers and brands.

Germany is also developing its first offshore gas field in the North Sea. There are two reservoirs of over 66 billion cubic metres.

In April 1998, Germany passed its own Energy Law which provides the framework for third-party access.

Germany also intends to implement the EU directive on Natural Gas Liberalisation when it comes into force. Measures in this directive include the following:

1. Governments can choose between negotiated or regulated third-party access.

2. There will be a special procedure to check access refusals based on Take Or Pay (TOP).

3. An authority independent from the parties should be designed to handle disputes on access.

4. There should be separate accounts for gas transmission, distribution and storage and non-gas activities.

The Germans have also agreed to International third-party access (TPA) for electricity. This third-party access is an important feature. The Poles have only agreed to third-party access on both gas and electricity networks provided the source is in Poland. This contravenes the Directive.

## Nuclear

Nuclear power is an important element in the German energy mix and helps towards the country's ambitious greenhouse gas reduction targets. The use of nuclear energy is helping to avoid between 150 and 160 million tonnes of $CO_2$ emissions per year.

Germany has twenty nuclear power stations supplying about one third of the country's electricity. Many are large: they total 22,289 Mwe. Six are boiling water reactors. Thirteen are pressurised water reactors. All were built by Siemens. A further PWR has not operated since 1988 due to a licensing dispute. No new nuclear power station has been built since 1989. Generally however the German attitude to nuclear power is reasonably favourable. There are plans to build a class of Enhanced Pressurised Water Reactors, known as the European PWR, along with the French. Germany therefore differs sharply from Poland, where the opposition to nuclear power prevents any build at all and where consequently the emission of greenhouse and other gases is much greater per unit of electricity generated.

The present German Government is in theory anti-nuclear. In October 1999 talks took place aimed at phasing out nuclear power. If agreement is not reached, the Greens threaten unilateral curtailment of licences without compensation. However all Germany's operating nuclear power plants have unlimited licences with strong legal guarantees. Thus the main arm of the new Government, the SPD, though formally anti-nuclear, is ducking the issue somewhat by stating that their chief priority is to counter unemployment.

They are also doubtless considering Germany's commitment to a 21% reduction in greenhouse gases arising from the Kyoto accord. In 1998 the Federation of German Industries announced that the 'politically undisturbed operation of nuclear plants' was a prerequisite for its co-operation in reaching greenhouse gas emission targets. German public opinion seems to have swung towards nuclear energy over the past six years. A poll late in 1997 showed that 81% of Germans wanted nuclear plants to continue operating at the highest level for many years. This compares with a similar poll in 1991 when those in favour were 64%.

This pro nuclear attitude did not however extend to the Russian designed reactors of the former German Democratic Republic. All of them were shut down for safety reasons in 1990. There were four operating, a fifth being built, and a sixth much older and relatively small.

This shut down led to decommissioning and its associated costs.

The following are now being dismantled:

| | |
|---|---|
| Greifswald | 8 x 440 MW units. |
| Rheinsberg | 2 x 62 MW units. |
| Stendal | 2 x 1,000 MW units. |

Some old and small power stations in the West are also being decommissioned at a cost of 200 to 220 million DM per plant. This gives some warning of the costs to come when all the PWRs in the West reach the end of their lives.

There are also problems with radioactive waste. The repositories for high level waste are meant to be in a salt dome at Gorleben and at Ahaus, but there is as much opposition to this as there is to the British repository at Sellafield. A final statement will be made on Gorleben in 2005. However, low level waste described as 'waste with negligible heat content' seems to worry the Germans less than it does the British. There are 16 external waste interim storage facilities and three for spent fuel.

The option of reprocessing spent fuel is becoming less popular. Before 1994 it was indeed the only option allowed. Between 1994 and 1998 direct disposal and reprocessing became equally acceptable. But the policy of the present government is for direct disposal only: this despite firm contracts with BNFL and Cogema to reprocess.

Thirteen of Germany's nuclear power stations are licensed to burn MOX, the product of reprocessed fuel, yet the only MOX plant in Germany has never been allowed to operate.

Thus all MOX is imported.

Thus nuclear power in Germany has its problems. But these should not obscure the main point. This is that Germany has a large nuclear power programme and related industrial infrastructure. Nuclear plants are efficiently run and they constantly achieve very high load factors and have an exemplary safety record. There are no subsidies for nuclear power.

Poland has decided not to consider the building of any nuclear power stations before 2008.

Should she exceed EU emissions before then, however, she could do worse than to build earlier, on German lines.

## Lignite

The position is similar to that of Poland. Lignite is of low calorific value but inexpensive and unsubsidised. As mentioned above, the inefficient lignite mines in the East have either been closed down or modernised. The biggest development is a huge new open cast mine in North Rhine/Westphalia which is a surprising development in a country with such a strong green lobby.

## Hard Coal

Germany became the largest producer of hard coal in the European Union in 1994. This was mainly due to the rapid decrease in UK production. Germany's own production had been decreasing at an annual rate of 3% since 1973, leading to an overall cut in production of about one half. In 1996 production stood at 34.2 Mtoe, from a workforce of 85,200 at the end of that year.

The main coal mining area is the Ruhr. The seams are narrow, deep and steeply angled. The coal is harder to extract than either British or Polish coal. Until 1995 an agreement called the *Jahrhundertvertrag* stipulated that power stations must burn only German coal. This, as said above, costs around three times as much as imported coal. The greater cost was met by a levy on all electricity bills called the *Kohlepfennig*. This raised the price of electricity by 8.5%. In December 1994 the Federal Constitutional Court ruled that this special levy was inconsistent with Germany's Constitution. As a consequence, Parliament abolished the *Kohlepfennig* a year later. Thus, since January 1996, subsidies have been given directly to the coal mining industry and have been financed out of the federal budget. *This contravenes EU directives.* Domestic production is still 90 million tonnes, though imported coal has increased to 40 million tonnes.

The German government is still trying to reduce domestic production and the work force. The subsidy to each miner is equivalent to 66,000 DM. Therefore, the government offers substantial benefits to those who leave:

1. If a miner obtains a new job outside his normal place of work or residence he can claim travel and removal expenses and a compensatory payment if he has to retain two households.

2. He receives equalisation pay if his new wage is less than his old.

3. He receives a grant for retraining.

4. He is entitled to a waiting payment (*wartegeld*) if immediate alternative employment is not available.

5. If in receipt of insurance benefit he receives a lump sum redundancy payment.

Even so, estimates of assistance to German coal producers rose until 1994 and then fell slightly according to the IEA as follows:

| 1991 | 1992 | 1993 | 1994 | 1995 | 1996 |
|------|------|------|------|------|------|
| 157.9 | 170.6 | 177 | 223.4 | 206.8 | 203 |

(DM per tonne produced.)

These are still high in comparison with other EU countries. They are evidence of the strength of the hard coal mining industry. In the table below only Japanese subsidies are higher.

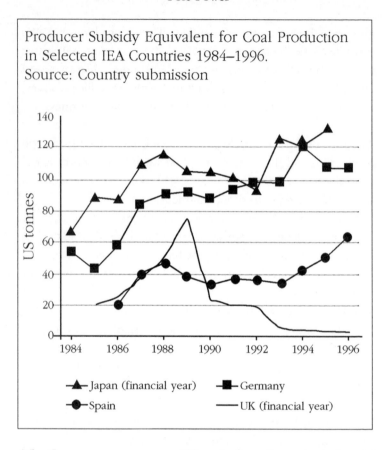

Producer Subsidy Equivalent for Coal Production in Selected IEA Countries 1984–1996.
Source: Country submission

The German government still lives in fear of massive industrial disruption in the Ruhr.

It is particularly remarkable that the miners in Germany should be so powerful when most of them are Gastarbeiter (guest workers), normally Turks. Whatever the nationality of the coal miners, the Energy Law which became effective on 1 January 1998 shows their power. It is an agreement on future coal subsidies on the basis of the following objectives:

1. To give the industry necessary security for long-term planning and a sustainable perspective until 2005.

2. To implement the adaptation process in a socially acceptable manner.

3. To preserve a viable and efficient mining industry with a total of 10 or 11 mines in 2005 (out of 18 mines in 1997). This production would cover more than 40% of the total German hard coal demand expected in 2005.

4. To maintain access to major deposits for future generations.

5. To preserve opportunities for the German mining equipment industry to experiment on its products.

So far as electricity generation is concerned, the forecast chart below shows coal to still be the main fuel in 2010.

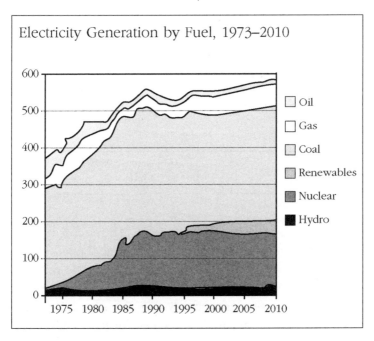

Source: IEA, *Energy Balances of OECD Countries* (Paris: OECD) and country submission.

**Electricity Prices**

The power of the deep mined coal industry guarantees that electricity will be relatively expensive in Germany. Indeed, the industrial consumer only pays more for his electricity in two other EU countries as the table below shows.

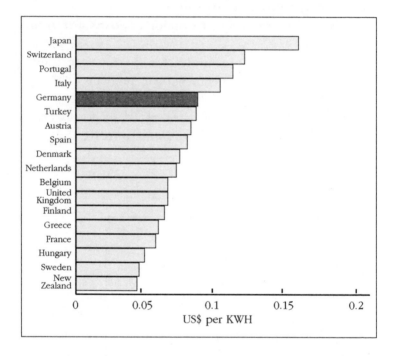

Other factors contribute to high prices. The electricity sector may be decentralised, but regional and local monopolies remain. There are exclusive concession contracts which do not allow competition. The overall dispatching system has not been based on the principle of merit order. Rather, the dispatch system of each electricity company has been organised to allow each company to favour its own power plants over other companies' plants, regardless of cost.

Before 1998 German electricity was the most expensive in Europe. Now it is at last coming down in price. According to the US Energy Information Service this reduction is quite substantial:

'Industrial prices are now down by 30 to 40% from their peak, and domestic prices should follow suit.'

However, smaller companies and new entrants to the market complain that the market is not yet truly free as the Grid and the RECs make it difficult for consumers to change suppliers.

Yet companies are advertising new energy packages. Marketing is becoming a key element. Price wars are driving down energy prices and spot markets are developing. Thus the Americans paint a mixed picture of German electricity.

Yet the only cheap fuel creating it is lignite. Both hard coal and nuclear are expensive. With expensive fuel, how can electricity be inexpensive? The only genuine way of reducing electricity prices is surely to switch to natural gas.

## Conclusion

The condition of the biggest energy market in the EU therefore lies midway between the liberalism of the UK and the state control of Poland. Though Germany's power is in some ways freer than British power, it does not have Britain's choice of fuels. For instance, it must import most of its natural gas. This strengthens the position of the indigenous hard coal industry, which is a loss leader. The lignite industry runs well without subsidy but it creates huge quantities of $CO_2$. The nuclear sector seems to run well, though it is naturally meeting with increased opposition from the present SPD/Green government. Renewables are of little consequence.

The hope for Germany, as for Poland, is a radical switch to natural gas.

# CHAPTER 13

## Poland's Transition Towards the EU

'Some people see the superiority of the "Chinese Way" in the fact that market reform preceded political democratisation.'

Thus writes Balcerowicz in working paper number 11 for the European Bank for Reconstruction and Development. He continues:

'They assert that by repeating the classic sequence "capitalism first, democracy later" they create a better chance of achieving both than the reverse order, as is happening in central and east European countries.'

However, once Europe had started the opposite sequence of 'democracy first, capitalism later' it was unstoppable as 'it takes less time to organise elections than to privatise the economy'. It is indeed easier to change politically than to change economically.

Thus does Balcerowicz, the architect of Poland's sea change in the early 1990s defend his method, often called Shock Therapy: immediate democratic reform and gradual economic reform, though I must comment that economic reform in Poland in the early 1990s was not that gradual and caused both massive unemployment and hyper inflation. But three years later the Poles themselves were arguing that Balcerowicz's tough medicine had been shown to be the best way forward.

Balcerowicz continues in this learned article to show how a change from command to market economy changes class structures and breeds the politics of envy. It is tempting to quote in extenso, but I will confine myself to one paragraph near the end as this explains the basic difference in attitude of the EU to Central Europe and vice versa.

'In the West...there appears to be a mistaken belief that the Western countries as a whole are somehow making an economic sacrifice if they open up their markets to poorer countries, including those in Central and Eastern Europe. The basic truth that both sides can benefit from freer trade...is strangely missing. In fact what is required from the West is not economic sacrifice but rather some courage and imagination on the part of the politicians which would measure up to the unprecedented changes that have happened in the East.'

From this viewpoint the conclusions of the European Council in Copenhagen, June 1993, may be considered somewhat patronising. These are the *Acquis* preconditions:

'The associated countries in central and Eastern Europe that so desire shall become members of the Union. Accession will take place as soon as a country is able to assume the obligations of membership by satisfying the economic and political conditions.

Membership requires:

1. That the candidate country has achieved stability of institutions guaranteeing democracy, the rule of law, human rights and respect for and protection of minorities.

2. The existence of a functioning market economy as well as the capacity to cope with competitive pressures and market forces within the Union.

3. The ability to take on the obligations of membership, including adherence to the aims of political, economic and monetary union.'

In 1995 the European Council met again in Madrid and stressed once more the importance of a market economy and the creation of a stable economic and monetary environment.

Specifically for Poland the Council decided on the following three medium term objectives:

1. Implement and enforce the Common Agricultural Policy.
2. Implement the EU Health and Safety at Work Directive.
3. Ensure equal opportunities for men and women.

The different attitudes of Balcerowicz and the Union go a long way to explaining friction that has arisen between the EU and Poland. The EU tends to regard pre-accession support of Poland as an act of philanthropy, if not of charity. But Poland in return (Pawlak) talks of 'Our contemporary pro Europeanism turning into an ideology of servility towards the wealthy capitalist world'. He adds:

'The EU appear to suggest that we should liquidate Polish agriculture altogether.' He believes that the EU 'demand a great deal but give little concrete in return'.

Actually the EU have provided considerable finance for Poland in terms of pre-accession funding. Whether one regards this money as a shrewd investment, or more in the light of a donation to Oxfam, it is still money, and hard currency at that. But dealing with this fascinating clash of cultures I am not claiming infallibility for the EU. They too made mistakes.

The EU decided quite quickly that simple unconditional gifts of lump sums to the East could end up in the wrong hands. An unfortunate side effect of the collapse of Communism was the growth of a new gangster or Mafia class. Many of its members worked themselves into positions of power.

As Bideleux and Jeffries put it in *A History of Eastern Europe*, 'It is alright when the nomenklatura kill each other, but it is not alright when they bribe each other.'

To avoid misappropriation, Brussels, surely itself the epitome of bureaucracy, decided that Eastern Aid should be directed towards a series of Committee reports by Western experts. This led to the Polish accusation that EU aid to the East was actually EU aid to EU consultants.

In the early 1990s the EU refuted this accusation by the introduction of 'twinning'. One Western expert and one Pole became joint and equal partners in each sector. The area chosen was energy. The aim was to free up the whole field. Yet the Energy Restructuring Group was a disaster. They were never integrated. European experts arriving in Warsaw found that they had not been given offices. Therefore the coal expert, who was British, thought it best to decamp to the coal restructuring office in Katowice. This clearly separated him from the main committee, but the American expert, on privatisation, was separated even more as he 'hardly ever showed up, since there was not enough work to do on privatisation' (Wolfgang Mostert Associates Report, 1995). This project was one of the early beneficiaries of PHARE.

## PHARE

PHARE wrote a country Strategy Document for Poland. The final draft was published in November 1996. At that stage Poland's Energy Law had been drafted but not enacted and PHARE reported that seven aspects called for 'substantial changes within governmental energy policy goals'.

1. Settling property relationships and promoting legal conditions for increased flexibility in the energy sector.

2. Restructuring the mining sector (*n.b. not reducing the mining sector*).

3. Promoting competition within the sector, including free access to the grid.

4. Gradually bringing the fuel and energy sectors to market levels and creating a pricing system.

5. Developing a system to stimulate reasonable energy consumption and publishing a set of efficiency standards for high energy consumers

6. Meeting environmental protection standards at EU levels: i.e. air pollution, salinity of mining waters and solid waste from coal combustion *(a tall order)*.

7. Providing energy security at EU levels. That is, diversification of procurement sources, a system of strategic and trade reserves, and a new account settlement system. *(This last item possibly referring to the failure of coal-mines to pay taxes hitherto)*.

Whilst these seven goals could be criticised for being a shade too general, they are tough. Indeed, were they all to be part of the Energy Law, Poland would not be able to afford to implement them.

The PHARE document is a thorough 81-page piece of work. Some of its recommendations are cosmetic and actually mean very little. For instance:

'Maintenance of hard coal production at an economically justified level and a rational development of the power industry based on brown coal' *(who could possibly advocate the opposite: that is, an irrational development of the power industry based on brown coal?)*.

Others are costly, e.g.:

'Creation of a financial system that will make it possible to gain the investment means for the necessary modernisation and maintaining of strategic reserves of fuel.'

One is rather interesting:

'The reduction of sulphur dioxide is a top priority', as on page 79 of the document we learn that, 'with the exception of sulphur dioxide the emission of basic atmospheric pollutants in Poland per inhabitant is currently on the average level for EU countries.'

$SO_2$, therefore, is Poland's only bad gaseous pollutant. There is no need to spend large sums on removing Nox or methane.

Some suggestions are just wrong:

'Solution of the problem of the removal of saline water from mines. The mines that will not solve that problem will be closed.'

This is opposed to the Polish view that a closed coal-mine discharges more salt into the rivers than an open one.

Whatever its faults PHARE is the main source of funding for Poland. PHARE makes gifts.

Other organisations, such as the World Bank and the European Bank for Reconstruction and Development (EBRD), make loans.

PHARE's gifts are conditional on Poland demonstrating the expected benefits that will accrue from each, and of setting out a means of realising such benefits. The means could be quite specific. For instance, Poland might say 'Should we receive 20 million euros to modernise the Katowice Steel Works, British Steel (Corus) has guaranteed to provide another 30 million euros and take over this company, provided that the workforce is reduced by 8,000 people.'

In the past, Poland has not been specific enough about PHARE funds. There was, 'a lack of sufficient mature projects meeting the priorities of the accession partnership' (EU report on Poland's accession, Nov 98). Recognising this, the Directorate

General IA, Enlargement in Brussels actually withdrew 34 million euros of PHARE funding in 1998, to the chagrin of the Poles.

DGIA is quite robust about Polish funding. When I met them in June 99 they asked me 'Why should the Western taxpayer pay for the retraining of Polish miners?' They told me that EBRD and the World Bank had already *lent* 60 million euros for this purpose. They further criticised Poland for failing to spend sufficient money in 1998 to attain full EU membership. US$40 billion was required. Poland spent only US$1 billion. 'We should admit them to the EU on a taper, through a system of membership that both we and they can afford.'

They also remarked that of the 11 countries applying for EU membership, Poland was near the bottom. Be that as it may, PHARE did give Poland's coal sector 20 million euros in 1999.

Total PHARE assistance to Poland was as follows (in million euros):

1990:  180.8
1991:  197
1992:  200
1993:  225
1994:  208.8
1995:  174
1996:  203
1997:   ?
1998:  150
1999:  265
2000:  400

With additional sums of 350 million for environment and transport and 168 million for agriculture EU aid totalled 918 million euros in the first year of the new millennium.

Alan Mayhew was head of PHARE. When he left he became head of East European Studies at Sussex University. In his book *Recreating Europe* (Cambridge, 1998) he answers the question 'What's wrong with PHARE?' with this list:
1. Its procedures are cumbersome and slow.
2. Relations between Eastern Europe delegations and Brussels lead to inefficiency.
3. There's not enough money.
4. There is not enough conditionality. (And this despite the PHARE fine, mentioned above.)
5. There is political control over programme detail.

Mayhew's comments that PHARE is cumbersome and slow are echoed by the Polish Under Secretary of State for Energy, Pawel Samecki, in his evidence to House of Lords sub committee A on 16 June 1998. He comments on the PHARE fine. Answering Lord Barnett, chairman, he states that whilst the fine does 'reflect the lack of certain technical preparation on our side' he goes on, 'bureaucratic delays exist in the whole of PHARE: not just with regard to Poland. This was the beginnings of PHARE and the original sin of PHARE in a sense. These delays do occur. Especially in the past they did occur because of lengthy procedures, lots of levels of decision making in place, and lots of institutions and units within the Commission involved.'

(Barnett) 'So the system is at fault rather than any particular country or even the Commission?'

(Samecki) 'We have been advocating changes in the PHARE programme for many years.'

Criticism of the PHARE programme is not confined to Poland. A considerable debate arose between the European Parliament and the Commission. The Rapporteur of the Parliamentary Committee was the Labour MEP Dr Gordon Adam.

These are two items in his original report to the Commission:

'(The European Parliamentary Committee) calls for greater priority on energy within the PHARE programme and for a higher percentage of projects over 100,000 euros to be devoted to Energy Projects.'

'It calls for more practical steps to help the coal regions of central Europe to carry out the necessary restructuring and rationalisation of the coal sectors and the adoption of clean coal technologies.'

The Commission's reply:

'Concrete measures have already been adopted to assist the Central European countries in the field of coal restructuring. In the PHARE programme, studies have been carried out to evaluate the status of the coal sector especially in Poland, Czech Republic, Hungary, Romania and Bulgaria.'

Adam replied that no comprehensive co-ordinated coal sector programmes have been proposed or developed by the Commission, and he added that the European Regional Clean Coal Study (finalised in June 1997) was the first attempt to provide a comprehensive integrated approach to needs of coal sectors both from a regional and a national point of view. The recommendations of this study *should be treated with the utmost seriousness and urgency by the Commission* (my emphasis).

Thus there is dissension between Parliament and the Commission over energy and PHARE.

I cannot leave PHARE without mentioning two pieces of work undertaken by them of immense benefit. The first is the document on Convergence of Energy Policies in Eastern Europe, published on 28 June 1997 and actually written by the Netherlands Energy Research Foundation. This is the definitive work on Eastern energy and I will return to it.

The second is the PHARE monitoring station at Usti on the Elbe, in the Czech Republic, which I mentioned in Chapter 7 – Lignite. This measures SOX, Nox and particulate emissions from the three countries forming the black triangle; Germany, Czech Republic and Poland. There are 43 monitoring stations reporting to Dariusz Kobus, head of the station.

The news is good from Poland's point of view. Overall emissions are down by 80% since 1989.

There are many international pre-accession organisations helping Poland that I list below.

The World Bank is the largest of the International Financial Institutions (IFIs). It funds both infrastructure and restructure developments. It also funds schemes designed to cushion social damage: in Poland's case it has lent US$200 million to restructure the coal industry.

It is worth saying more about the European Bank for Reconstruction and Development which was formed by Mitterand in 1991. Thirty-nine countries belong to it. It is London based and its original capital was 10 billion euros.

Accused of spending more money on itself than on its clients, the President Jacques Allali resigned in 1993 to be succeeded by Larosiere. It is disliked by the USA who see it as duplicating the functions of the World Bank.

It disbursed the following amounts in the following years:

1992: 127 million euros
1993: 409 million euros
1994: 988 million euros
1995: 988 million euros.

It funds energy service companies, or ESCOs. These are private companies which offer a range of energy saving measures and take a proportion of the savings as their fee.

The European Investment Bank (EIB) seems similar to the EBRD, but with only one third of its funds.

JOULE-THERMIE is concerned with dissemination and demonstration of new energy technologies.

SAVE serves a role analogous to that of THERMIE but in the field of energy conservation.

SYNERGY exists to promote improved energy management.

ALTENER promotes renewable energy such as wind farms.

# CHAPTER 14

## The Acquis (I): Energy

The first two European treaties after the Second World War concerned energy. The first was the European Coal and Steel Treaty and the second was Euratom or 'Atoms for Peace'. The motives that powered both were to make World War III impossible. With pooled coal, steel and nuclear energy a further conflict could surely not take place. These treaties preceded the Treaty of Rome, The European Economic Community and any idea of federalism or surrender of sovereignty in the member states which were then France, Germany, Italy and Benelux.

Today we have the technical miracle of the West European Grid. Throughout the European Union each and every contributing power station is exactly synchronised in its A/C phasing: 50 cycles per second. Demand is not constant. It is generally higher in winter but there are many more ephemeral variations caused by unexpected cold snaps or half time in a football match on television when the switching on of a million electric kettles will cause a very rapid one gigawatt surge. Thus the EU power stations and the Grid must load follow. They manage to do so within the parameters of 50.5 cycles and 49.5. This is as difficult as driving a vehicle up hill and down dale, through mist fog and ice, through heavy traffic at a speed never more than 50.5 mph or less than 49.5. Thus, regarding Poland and the *Acquis*, it would appear at first sight that Poland's compliance with the energy Policy would be her hardest goal.

But this is not so. With the exception of the environment with which I deal in the following chapter the other hurdles that Poland must clear to comply with EU energy are relatively modest.

This is because national self-interest took over after the coal, steel and atomic treaties mentioned above. After the war there was a shortage of generating capacity and this ensured that the two treaties would never develop into a Common Energy Policy similar to the Common Agricultural Policy. The uncertainty of Middle Eastern oil supplies led the UK to ensure its own supply, by forming BP, for instance.

There was also a hard held belief that home produced energy was the most secure. This led the coal producing countries to go to almost any lengths to support and subsidise their own coal industries. Those countries are the UK, Germany and Spain. In the UK our domestic fuel supply turned out to be quite insecure as the miners recognised the power of their position and held the country to ransom by striking. Mrs Thatcher beat the miners in the early 80s. But it was not total victory. Even now, with all mines privatised, the Labour Government is subsidising our largest mining company, RJB, to the tune of £100 million.

Thus the Poles, with their own coal mining difficulties, will be able to argue that what is sauce for the goose is sauce for the gander. Both Germany and Spain still subsidise their coal-mines to an extent even greater than the UK. It will be hard for the EU to deny Poland admission for reasons of subsidised coal.

France poses a different problem to the EU and further weakens the goal of a Common Energy Policy. She can only maintain her electricity industry by keeping Electricité de France as a monopoly. Her power is principally nuclear. Capital intensive, it would quickly go under if there was a genuine free-for-all in the Union featuring hundreds of gas turbines and cheap coal from Australia. For these reasons France must deny third-party access to her grid (though she has third-party access to other countries' grids as she exports nuclear powered electricity to Austria via Germany, for instance). Poland at present allows TPA provided that the generator is based in Poland. This contravenes both spirit and letter of the Single European Energy Market, but once again Poland can play a trump card in her accession negotiations. This is the French card.

The field of third-party access is one of the few areas where Brussels is developing a competence. Brussels requires the National Regulators to decide on the best system of foreign access to the Grids. Thus it is known as *regulated* TPA. Even the French cannot simply dismiss this. So they have come up with alternatives: *negotiated* TPA and the concept of the Single Buyer.

## Negotiated TPA

To explain how this works I will imagine that Germany wishes to sell electricity to Spain via the French Grid. The method is to arrange a price acceptable to the Spanish and acceptable also to Electricité de France. It is not therefore a free market price. It highlights one of the central problems of electricity trading. He who owns the grid controls the price. This is the case in France, and in Poland. It can be altered by the regulator provided that he has sufficient power and money. Indeed, all over Europe it is difficult to avoid a monopoly in electricity selling. In the UK it is more a cartel of generators than the grid itself. But it would seem that a common feature is that the regulator is fighting the industry. Where in the world is there a genuine free market in electricity?

The above global arguments are relevant to the *Acquis* since they make Poland's accession easier, through the faults of present EU members.

## The Single Buyer

Suppose, as above, that Germany wishes to sell to Spain via the French Grid. She can do so under this system provided that she sells at the agreed Spanish price but does not sell directly to Spain. Rather she must sell to France. The French Grid are bound to charge for conveying the electricity onwards to Spain. Whilst Germany and Spain have negotiated a free market price, that price is known to the French and it is tempting for France to undercut Germany by making a cheaper offer to Spain. The French can also refuse access due to lack of capacity.

The Commission has accepted the principle of the Single Buyer and of negotiated TPA with the proviso that, 'They must have an equal economic effect and lead to an equal level of market access'. This is vague to say the least.

It is true that the French are actually very frightened of a single electricity market. It is also true that they are setting a bad example to new countries wishing to join the EU.

Other coal producing countries: the UK, Germany and Spain, are little better. Regarding the TPA directive in general it seems likely that some of the current member states will opt for the following:

France and Italy: Single Buyer.
Denmark, Greece and Belgium: negotiated TPA.
Sweden, Finland and the UK: regulated TPA.

It is easy to understand Polish resentment when she claims that there is one set of rules for entrants and another set for members.

The Commission did establish a 'Common Rules' directive in 1996, much fought over and much revised since the original proposal of 1992. This incorporated a price transparency directive, originally proposed in 1990. Its aim was to ease competition by enabling industrial users of electricity to get some idea of what their competitors were paying in other member states.

Brussels has succeeded in one area concerning security of supply. It is that each member country must hold a reserve of 90 days oil supply. This is to guard against future crises in the Middle East. This will be difficult and costly for Poland, though there is flexibility here. Greece has managed to include in her 90-day supply all oil being shipped around the world in Greek tankers.

The Energy Directorate in Brussels, DGXVII/TREN, has produced an important paper called Synergy Poland 1996 that I will return to. DGXVII/TREN is actually rather weak when it acts on its own. It has even been suggested that it be amalgamated with another Directorate, as in the UK, where the old Department of Energy is now just a branch of the Department of Trade and Industry.

DGXVII/TREN becomes stronger when it works alongside other Directorates: DGXI ENVIRONMENT as I will show later, but also Leon Britten's Directorate General IV: Competition. If the French are called to book it would more likely originate in an attack on lack of competitive practices than in any matter which is the direct concern of DG TREN.

It is significant that there was no Energy Chapter agreed at Maastricht.

## The Acquis II: General

The *Acquis* itself would need a book to itself. It consists of thousands of directives and regulations. It is not specific to Poland. However some Community Documents are specific and the three most useful are:

1. *The Official Journal of the European Communities* 29 June 98, on Accession Partnerships.

2. *The Commission Opinion on Poland's Application for Membership*, known as Agenda 2000. This was written in July 1997 but updated in November 1998.

3. *Synergy Poland*, written by DGXVII/TREN in 1996. This addresses Poland's energy problems and the Energy Law of 1997 and is therefore most relevant.

## 1. The Official Journal of the European Communities, June 1998, Accession Partnerships

Pre-accession strategy:

'The PHARE programme is the main instrument of the pre-accession strategy. This is how it should work: each year the Commission will sign with Poland a financing memorandum in which Poland will undertake to meet a number of priorities and the Commission will undertake to contribute financially to their realisation.'

The PHARE moneys will be split. Around 30% will go to institution building, and 70% to investment support.

Under institution building, support will be implemented through training, technical assistance and twinning of administrations in Poland with their opposite numbers in the member States.

Priority areas will be finance, agriculture, justice, environment and home affairs.

Under investment support, PHARE will cover agriculture, regional development, and human and intellectual capital. It will also cover compliance with community norms; with particular regards to the environment, industry, occupational safety and health, transport and telecommunications.

It will also co-finance large scale infrastructure and small and medium sized enterprises.

However, financial assistance to Poland will depend on the maturity of projects proposed by the Polish Government. If Poland cannot fulfil its indicative commitments the allocation will be reduced accordingly. It was on these grounds that PHARE withheld 34 million euros of aid to Poland in 1998.

## 2. Agenda 2000

This document is generally pro Polish. At the start it states:

'Poland shows a realistic, constructive and open attitude to solving problems which arise, and an awareness of the dangers of protectionism and of the importance of tackling difficulties through negotiation.'

Freedom of expression, asylum and minority rights get clean bills of health. There is justified criticism of farming. The document deals with every aspect of accession to the Union and is some 120 pages long. In order to avoid a chapter of 120 pages I prefer to select from it passages relevant to energy, starting with Agenda 2000's general statement that, 'industry is the driving force behind recovery'.

However:

'Coal mining is recognised as a particularly troubled sector where prices and wages have increased faster than in the rest of the economy'. Agenda 2000 follows this with the pious hope that 'coal will increasingly be substituted by imports of natural gas from Russia'.

Further criticisms of coal follow:
'Price setting in the coal market is distorted because coal-mines are still allowed to run at a loss.'

Coal export subsidy is criticised. State aid is not sufficiently transparent. Aid is granted indirectly through tax relief and debt write-offs. It is therefore quite hard to quantify. Certain aid measures are clearly not compatible with EU accession.

Regarding Polish forecasts on the contraction of the coal industry, it is interesting to see which targets have been met a mere three years after the writing of Agenda 2000. The Hard Coal Restructuring Agency in Katowice forecast a widespread reduction in the workforce. This has indeed occurred. The agency also forecast widespread closure of coal-mines. In fact few coal-mines have closed and the agency's further forecast that 'remaining mines will be profitable by 1998 and debt repayment will start' was sadly wrong.

But Agenda 2000 concludes that, 'Poland should be able to comply with the rest of the energy *Acquis* in the medium term, though this will require, *inter alia*, some work on state intervention in the coal sector.'

### 3. The DGXVII Paper Synergy Poland, 1996
This document, written a year earlier than Agenda 2000, is more critical of Poland's energy sector. It lists Poland as having these key characteristics:
1. A heavy reliance on domestic coal for electricity and heat generation.

2. A heavily subsidised coal sector which is currently undergoing restructuring.

3. A large inefficient generation plant in need of modernisation.

4. A near total dependence on imported oil.

5. An increasing demand for natural gas.

6. Severe environmental problems and inefficiency.

*Acquis* areas in which Poland will find compliance difficult are politely called 'bottlenecks'.

The document was written before Poland passed her Energy Law. Much faith is placed in this future piece of legislation.

These are the bottlenecks:

1. Price fixing agreements between coal companies.

2. No legally binding public service obligations.

3. Subsidies and cross subsidies in the heat sector.

4. State aid to the hard coal industry.

5. No international third-party access. No legislation relating to the transit of natural gas and electricity through Poland.

6. No legislation about standards, labelling and energy efficiency (SAVE).

7. General price fixing is widespread and does not comply with the European Coal and Steel (ECSC) treaty.

8. The Polish Power Grid Company and the Polish Oil and Gas Company have *de facto* exclusive rights.

9. The Ministry of Finance sets maximum prices that can be charged for electricity. If the RECs' costs exceed these prices they are re-imbursed by Government.

*(Both bottlenecks 8 and 9 seem to have been removed with the freeing up of the gas and electricity markets in 2000, my italics.)*

10. Poland will continue to subsidise the coal sector beyond 2000.

11. Poland does not have the capacity to store 90 days of oil supplies.

12. Boilers do not meet EU standards.

DG TREN then continue to list these specific objectives for the Energy Law.

1. Secure Poland's supply of energy and fuels.

2. Achieve efficiency in the production and use of energy and fuels.

3. Develop competitive conditions in the energy industries.

4. Protect consumers' interests.

5. Minimise costs.

The Energy Law was finally passed in December 1997. It had been looked on as the panacea to all Poland's energy problems, including those of the *Acquis*.

These were its main features:

1. It created a framework for a private energy sector.

2. It established an independent regulatory body, the Energy Regulatory Authority (ERA, whose President is Juchniewicz).

3. It listed the types of activities that require a licence under the Law:

Production of electricity and fuels.

Transmission of electricity and fuels.

Trade in electricity and fuels.

4. It imposed basic criteria on the applicant for a licence. For instance the applicant must have an office in Poland. He must have sufficient funds for the activity in question. He must have the appropriate technical capability and employ suitable persons.

5. Licences are issued for periods of not less than ten and not more than fifty years. The ERA can withdraw a licence

under certain circumstances. These are described only in general terms and leave grounds for uncertainty.

6. The Law provides that the licence is conditional upon the licensee providing some sort of guarantee or security to cover environmental damage.

7. The Law imposed third-party access on generation and distribution. But it only applied to fuels and electricity produced in Poland. It therefore does not comply with the EU TPA Energy Directive.

The *AGENDA 2000* update in November 1998 is far less sanguine about Poland than the original document. Of the Energy Law:

'It created a basis for the progressive approximation with the EU's internal energy market rules. However, most of the secondary legislation necessary to make the Energy Law effectively operational is still awaited.'

On State aid it states:

'It is regrettable that Poland's commitments to transpose and implement the *Acquis*...have not been fulfilled, since this is a short term priority in the Accession Partnership.'

Michael Davies of Allen and Overy, Warsaw, sees the Energy Law as controversial. Those involved in it fall into two camps: those who consider that the Law does not sufficiently protect Polish interests and those who see it too tightly drawn for proper foreign participation. He also believes that the figure quoted in it to fund infrastructure of US$15 billion is not realistic. He prefers the Algemene Bank Nederland/AMRO bank figure of US$45 billion which is three times as much.

# CHAPTER 15

## The Acquis and the Environment

The *Acquis* consists of 31 sections or chapters. Number 22 is 'The Environment'. In September 1999 Poland sent her first negotiating position paper to Brussels. She asked for transition periods for fourteen directives. This is the highest number requested by any acceding country.

I had a meeting with Directorate General Environment on June 20, 2000 and they are refusing to accept two transition periods, the Hazardous Waste Directive and the Nature Protection Directive. Regarding the other twelve, the hurdles Poland must overcome are still considerable, even though transition periods will be allowed.

For instance, there is the problem of saline discharges into the Baltic from the Vistula. The salt originates in Silesia's coal-mines. I have said before that the Vistula is actually more salty than the Baltic Sea itself. This is quite unacceptable to those EU countries on the Baltic; Germany, Denmark, Sweden and Finland. They would like a clean Baltic.

There is a considerable problem with the Large Combustion Plant Directive (LCPD). This was first introduced in draft in 1983. It proposed drastic reductions in the emissions of $SO_2$, Nox and particulates from plants with an output greater than 50 MW thermal. That is, using 1980 as a baseline, a 60% reduction for $SO_2$, 40% for Nox and 40% for particulates.

The EU requires all boilers built since 1987 to comply with the Directive. The Polish position is that since they passed an

Emissions Act in 1990 the LCPD should only apply to boilers built after 1990. This is not acceptable to the EU, as any boiler built between 1987 and 1990 would be free of emission controls. It could in theory pump out huge quantities of toxic gases in perpetuity. Even with boilers undergoing a complete overhaul since 1990 the Poles argue that an overhaul does not make the boiler 'new'. It is still an old boiler, subject only to emission standards obtaining before the Large Combustion Plant Directive.

There is a problem with the Integrated Prevention of Pollution Control Directive (IPPC). This is a single framework directive affecting emissions to air, water and earth. This directive should have been implemented on all new installations by October 1999. The Poles wish for a postponement until accession. On existing installations the IPPC will come into force in 2007. The Poles have asked for a postponement till 2010. This directive is important as it insists on BAT, or best available technology.

There are other problems with the Drinking Water Directive and the Urban Waste Water Directive. DG XI, Environment told me that in general the Poles were light on timetables, investment strategies, source of funds and institutional structures. They forecast that there will be a low level of compliance from Poland and it is likely that there will be court actions.

In Brussels they believe that Poland is calling the European Union's bluff, as there will be no enlargement if Poland is excluded.

\* \* \*

It is clear that the authors of Agenda 2000 understand the problem of immediate compliance and are in favour of gradualism. They write:

'For the environment, very substantial efforts will be needed, including massive investment and strengthening of the administrative capacity to enforce legislation. Full compliance with the *Acquis* could only be expected in the long term and would require increased levels of public expenditure.'

Even today, after clean-up, the 4,000 megawatt lignite power station at Belchatow still emits as much $SO_2$ as Sweden, Norway and Denmark combined.

The definitive statement on the environment in Agenda 2000, runs as follows:

'The Community's Environmental Policy, derived from the Treaty, aims towards sustainability based on the integration of environmental protection into EU sectoral policies, preventive action, the polluter pays principle, fighting environmental damage at source, and shared responsibility.'

'The *Acquis* in its 200 legal acts covers a wide range of matters, including water and air pollution, management of waste and chemicals, biotechnology, radiation protection and nature protection. Member states are required to ensure that an Environmental Impact Assessment is carried out before development consent is granted for certain public and private projects.'

To comply with all the above, the Poles have another Environment Act in the pipeline. However, DG Environment are wary of it as they fear that it may be as short of specific measures as the 1997 Energy Act was.

DG Environment told me in June 1999:

'The Poles are passing a very broad framework Law dealing with the whole environment. The time scale for passing this is slipping and may not be in this Parliament. However the Poles are using it as a foil to EU suggestions that specific measures should be taken. Thus grandiose theories permit Poles to avoid specifics.'

DG Enlarge in their Agenda 2000 sequel of November 1998 are just as critical. They write:

'Environment: most sectors still present a very low level of approximation especially in the noise, chemicals, air and water sectors. The overall framework is poorly developed and it is hard to see how much progress can be made in the short term. Poland's national programme for the adoption of the *Acquis* needs to be considerably improved and it should cover the whole of the *Acquis* including clear transposition and implementation dates for each EU legal act.'

In the last chapter I described how the members of the EU were requiring the Poles to adopt a set of energy principles which they were not adopting themselves, for instance: unsubsidised coal-mines and free third-party access to the Grid. I argued that the Poles might successfully negotiate only partial compliance in these areas on the basis of the level playing field.

I suggested that when considering the environmental aspects of the energy *Acquis* the EU might be laying down firmer conditions, given the greater power of several Directorates working together. This is indeed so but the development of the EU's regard for the environment has been piecemeal and even the definition of pollution has been changing throughout the twentieth century.

Taking the example of the United Kingdom, the earliest instance of energy pollution was visual. The chains of electricity pylons forming our National Grid were thought to ruin the countryside. Pollution from power stations was less important. Power and coal were almost synonymous. Power stations were bound to be coal fired up to the Second World War.

In 1954 the UK passed the Clean Air Act. This concerned soot from household chimneys. It was not about noxious gases such as sulphur dioxide and it was not really targeted at power stations since the amount of soot, or particulates, emitted by them was very low compared to that from millions of ordinary chimneys. We did not really admit that sulphur dioxide was a problem until the mid 1980s. Other EU countries, downwind of us, had seen the problem 10 years earlier. Acid rain and the concomitant death of pine forests in Scandinavia forced us to become signatories to the first piece of EU sulphur legislation: The Large Combustion Plant Directive.

The UK delayed: asking for scientific proof of the ecological effects of acid rain and for the development of clean coal technologies that were less costly. As a result we did not have to meet the high reduction targets set for Northern Europe.

These used 1980 as base line and set $SO_2$ reductions of 40% by 1993, 60% by 1998 and 70% by 2003 for Germany, France and the Netherlands. Germany had installed much flue gas desulphurisation equipment and so was able to meet these targets. The Netherlands were mainly burning natural gas and France was mainly nuclear.

The UK, Italy, Spain and Denmark were given lower targets in view of their greater difficulty and cost in reducing emissions.

The UK was required to retrofit 12 gigawatts of capacity with FGD. Actually we only fitted half of this, at Drax, as we switched away from coal burning to natural gas and managed to achieve our reduction by that means.

It has been argued that the Large Combustion Plant Directive was motivated mainly by the desire to create a level playing field. One country generating power that had been cleaned up at great expense by removing $SO_2$ could clearly be undercut by another country that had not removed its $SO_2$.

It is also still argued that acid rain is a figment of the Greens' imagination and that if it exists it does not really damage trees anyhow. This argument is most likely bogus, but there is something dated about acid rain: a problem of the 70s and 80s that has been solved perhaps, if it ever existed. Public memory is quite short and the acid rain worries have now given way to those of global warming.

Global warming is even vaguer territory since carbon dioxide is not a toxic gas. We need $CO_2$ in our atmosphere since a certain amount of $CO_2$ makes the globe habitable. Without it we would freeze to death. At the other extreme we would boil to death if we had as much $CO_2$ as does the planet Venus. The big question is whether we are pumping sufficient $CO_2$ into our atmosphere to make any difference to the overall temperature. 70% of the world is not doing so, for it is water. Does what we do in the remaining 30% raise the global temperature? The answer is most likely yes, albeit at a slow rate. That is just based on a series of unproved scientific assumptions.

EU legislation is based on the precautionary principle: the notion that where no scientific certainty exists about damage, precaution demands that policy is framed on the basis that such damage is likely. The $CO_2$ fora have not been within the EU, but in Rio, Kyoto and Buenos Aires. The EU has agreed to limit emissions within its own territories at these conferences, but the conferences themselves have not come up with any legislation as specific as the Large Combustion Plant Directive.

The EU has also proposed a carbon tax. It was to start at US$1 per barrel of oil equivalent, rising by US$1 a year to US$10 per barrel. 50% was to be levied on the heat content of the fuel and 50% on the carbon content. Initially it was to be carbon only, but once more national self-interests prevailed in the Council of Ministers. The final shape of the tax is not very satisfactory. It would reduce industrial and household emissions more than power station and transport emissions. Overall reduction is reckoned to be 3.5% by 2000 but this is more than offset by a 21% rise in transport emissions alone over the same period.

The EU as a whole is doing quite well on $CO_2$ targets, but this is due to the policies of the UK and Germany. There is a Department of Environment, Transport and the Regions (DETR) climate change document arguing that the EU 'bubble' of 1998 should be converted into a legally binding commitment on member states. It would then become apparent that Denmark, allocated a 21% reduction, has achieved a 17% increase. Ireland: allocated a 13% reduction is up 21%. Austria: a 13% reduction is up 12%. The Netherlands: a 6% reduction is up 12%. Belgium, a 7.5% reduction is up 14%. Spain: a 15% reduction is up 28%.

There are EU programmes in place to reduce $CO_2$ emissions by 3-4.5% (SAVE) and to increase renewables from 4% to 8% (ALTENER). Both are poorly funded.

In general the EU has held back on its carbon tax, due to fears of high unemployment and losing international competitiveness and because there is a continuing lack of scientific consensus regarding the inevitability, timing and effects of global climate change.

Thus in the environmental part of the *Acquis* it is important to remember that many of our concerns about toxic gases and more so of non toxic gases such as $CO_2$ are of quite recent origin. Nor is the track record of both the Commission and the member countries whiter than white. Though no one has broken the rules, as is the case in the preceding chapter, they have certainly bent them and it ill behoves the Commission to be high handed in its dealings with Poland.

This sort of attitude by the Commission is criticised by Kirsty Hughes in her piece, 'A most exclusive club' in the *Financial Times* of 26 August 1998:

'The Commission fails to acknowledge the impact it is inevitably having on the transition process. It sees the deteriorating and increasingly fractious relationship with Poland as entirely of Poland's own making. Indeed the view is heard in Brussels that the deterioration is welcome, forcing the Poles to face up to reality. Tones of sibling rivalry can increasingly be heard: resentment perhaps at the growing confidence and assertiveness of this dynamic new regional player in the middle of Europe. Meanwhile, attitudes not unfamiliar in the UK are being heard in Poland; 'Poland will not go to the EU on bended knee' is a common phrase, as is 'coming back from Brussels bloodied but unbowed'.'

It is important to see how Poland's own State Inspectorate of Environmental Protection reported on the environment on 17 June 1999.

First it lists the reduction rates in tonnes of $SO_2$, Nox and particulates achieved between 1988 and 1999:

$SO_2$ from 4.2 millons to 2.3 million.

NOX from 1.5 million to 1.1 million.

Particulates from 3.5 million to 1.4 million.

It follows with two lists of key results:

Good:

1. Contaminating discharges to rivers have been significantly reduced resulting from implementation of a large number of new sewage treatment facilities.

2. A distinct improvement of surface flowing water quality has been evidenced over the recent years. The length of excessively polluted rivers has decreased by circa 50%.

3. Significant reduction in nuisance of noise from large industrial sources has been observed.

4. Forest condition has improved since 1995.

Bad:

1. No systematic solution to the hazardous waste problem.

2. No municipal waste selective collection and utilisation system.

3. Low utilisation rate of industrial waste.

4. Emission of pollutants from municipal and mobile sources.

5. Discharge of untreated sewage from large cities.

6. Discharge of salinated water from hard coal-mines.
7. Effect of motorisation growth on noise levels in cities.

The Poles identify and separate their problems. But this does not prevent the Commission from stating in general: 'Poland's national programme for the adoption of the *Acquis* does not propose target dates for the transposition and implementation of important framework legislation. It is hard to see how much progress can be made in the short term.'

I will now mention an important specific that could be called the Small Combustion Plant Directive. Quoting from DG TREN's Synergy paper,

'Smaller heat-only boilers with low stacks and individual coal fired residential heating units are particularly problematic as they are not subject to any controls, fees or fines and create major problems in dense urban areas. There are plans to replace small boilers with small CHP plants with assistance from the World Bank. The Polish Government has adopted the programme 'Government Policy of Energy Efficiency in the Housing Sector'. The programme includes the insulation of 2.4 million dwellings. Funding will be obtained from commercial banks with a requirement that 20% of the project be funded by the developer. The Polish Energy Foundation, KAPE *(Marina Coey, see above, page 127)* will administer a fund that will guarantee 50% of the loans which will be offered at preferential rates. In order to qualify for the fund a feasibility study will be required together with an energy audit conducted by a qualified auditor.'

Thus Poland plans to increase the efficiency of small boilers and at the same time reduce the need for heat by better insulation. This area may seem undramatic when compared to the installation of fluidised beds at Turow, but it is actually more important. It is also harder to enforce. But could Poland make her domestic consumption and insulation as good as that of Western Europe she would the more easily comply with the *Acquis* as well as guarantees given at Rio and Kyoto.

This brings me on to Poland's $CO_2$ emissions. They should raise no problems so far as the *Acquis* is concerned. Poland can actually increase emissions and still be in accord with the EU proposed $CO_2$ maxima for 2010.

Indeed Poland fears that her emissions might increase simply because she has joined the Union. I refer here to all emissions: $SO_2$, Nox and particulates as well as $CO_2$. Her fears are based on the fact that she will be on the periphery of the Union and that the main polluting industries of Western Europe may be tempted to move their dirtiest factories eastward.

However, pollution will surely be better than in the 1980s, when Poland was on the periphery of the Soviet Union. In fact the most polluted countries are likely to be those just outside the Union: that is, the Ukraine, Belorus and Turkey. Poland's fears must be groundless.

Thus, regarding the environmental aspects of the *Acquis,* there is not perfect harmony between Poland and Brussels. Both sides feel that the other is producing generalised statements that are short on specifics. From my trips to Poland I know that the Poles believe that Western Europe's impression of Poland is ten years out of date. But it is still the case that Poland needs 7.3 times as much energy to produce one unit of GDP as does the West.

# CHAPTER 16

## The Future of Polish Energy

At the end of the millennium Poland's energy sector was still State controlled in all but name.

The common description of any energy source, be it mine or power station, is 'a joint stock company wholly owned by the Treasury'. There are signs of breaking the mould. Some CHP stations, PAK and Polaniec power stations are now privatised. But change is happening more slowly than forecast. In 1990 the prediction was that the whole energy sector would be in private hands by 1993.

As well as a reluctance to sell, (for this does upset a command economy system that has existed for the last 50 years), there is also a reluctance by the West to buy. The Polish plant is simply old fashioned, dirty and labour intensive. Michael Davies of Allen and Overy set the figure for modernising all of it: US$45 billion is part of the huge sum that means that the cost of Poland's accession to the EU will exceed the total cost of all acceding countries to date.

In this country I asked Richard Budge of RJB Mining if he was tempted to buy Polish coal-mines. He replied that he was not, with some vigour. He is bringing a lawsuit against the Poles for dumping subsidised coal on the UK market.

The first requirement for a complete transformation in Poland's energy sector is strong government. Strong government can be tough with vested interests, as was our own in the 80s. At the moment Poland has a weak Government: a loose conglomeration of Solidarity Action Parties now in a minority since the split with Balcerowicz's Freedom Party. The President, Kwasniewski, is a Communist. His party, the SLD, is the favourite to win the general election in January 2001.

It is all too easy for a country such as ours to criticise Polish attempts at democracy when they have only had ten years to develop it, whilst we can trace its development back nearly 800 years to Magna Carta.

A possible way ahead for Poland would be regional government. The largest of the 17 voivodships is Silesia. It has an electorate of 5 million. Thus the Silesian Parliament represents more people than our Scottish Parliament does. However, there is no sign as yet that Poland is going the way of Germany with its Länder Governments.

The Government apart, the 1997 Energy Act has given considerable power to the regulator, Juchniewicz. It is for him to decide how coal should be bought by the power stations. He has a duty to deliver electricity to the consumer at the cheapest market price. That this is more than the old price is due to the heavy subsidy of both coal and electricity by the Communists which led to the tradition that energy was as good as free. In turn this led to a waste of energy in both production and consumption.

Juchniewicz therefore must raise prices to realistic levels. He is threatened by the Government and the National Grid for doing so, but the threats are empty because no one can remove Juchniewicz from office until his term expires in 3 years. A third of the prices will be determined on the new Energy Exchange in any event.

The head of the grid, Zmijewski, criticises the regulator for raising prices too much. So does Szlazak, the former Minister for Mines. But these gentlemen cannot have it both ways. If Juchniewicz is to fulfil his brief he should be allowed to introduce foreign TPA to the grid. This is forbidden by the 1997 Energy Law. But it would cheapen electricity. He should also be allowed to authorise the building of coastal power stations which would run on imported coal bought at the world price.

The regulator could, entirely legally, grant permission for a Pole to build a new power station at Gdansk, run it on imported coal and force the Grid to carry the power generated. The Energy Law allows TPA provided it is Polish.

It is obvious that the Government would prevent this. They would fear a miners' strike and could doubtless produce figures to show that running a station on imported coal actually cost more than domestic if redundancy payments to miners were included.

In contrast, Balcerowicz's solution is to close the mines and pull down every power station, then start again with Combined Cycle Gas Turbines. These would run off Russian, Norwegian, Dutch and North African gas. Poles naturally fear for security of supply if the supplier is foreign. In fact, a domestic supply is not secure if its workforce is liable to withhold its labour. The Russian programme, Gazprom, is independent of Russian politics. It is a state within a state and will continue to export gas westward no matter who is in power. Russia needs hard currency. Having said that, it is fairly obvious that the Balcerowicz plan will not be implemented. It is unrealistic to expect Europe's largest coal producer to stop production.

The way ahead will be the present way: modernisation of the mines and the power stations.

The workforce will decrease. So will production, but not drastically as the industry is becoming more efficient and the tonnes mined per worker are increasing. There will be nearly as much coal produced and Poland will seek to export the power generated by it to the West, thereby making it easier for Western countries to keep to Kyoto maxima.

Regarding the power stations, the Poles could hardly object if some Western fairy godmother offered to pull down the old and build anew. But this will not happen and I fear that there lies ahead a continuation of 'end of pipe' technology: a very expensive retrofit of existing power stations with FGD. There could also be more radical technology such as fluidised beds and integrated gasification combined cycle.

There is in addition the very real problem of the long-term contract between coal-mine and power station and between power stations and the Grid. The Government could break these contracts, but only by reimbursing the contracting parties, and for that it needs money. It can obtain money by exporting power to the West.

Indeed, there are three factors that will determine the fate of Poland's energy sector:
  1. What is politically desirable.
  2. What is financially possible.
  3. What is good for the environment.

Whilst I mentioned above that the Ministry of the Environment is relatively weak in Poland I must include Agenda 21, quite different from Agenda 2000 and a thoroughly sensible report by the National Foundation for Environmental Protection. As far back as 1991 the Sejm approved Agenda 21's National Environmental Policy which sets out the following objectives to be implemented by 2000:

1. Limiting of emissions of sulphur dioxide to 2.9 million tonnes.

2. Limiting of emissions of oxides of nitrogen to 1.3 to 1.4 million tonnes.

3. Reducing emissions of particulates by 50%.

4. Increasing the mean efficiency of dust removal to 96%.

5. Limiting emissions of volatile organic compounds, hydrocarbons, heavy metals and other pollutants.

6. The taking of action to combat global climate change 'that matches international efforts in this field', by 2010, by adopting these four measures:

a. Total elimination of coal fired burners in urban agglomerations and spa areas.

b. Introducing catalytic convertors to all cars produced and in use.

c. Reducing $SO_2$, Nox and $CO_2$ to levels agreed at international fora.

d. Eliminating CFCs and halons.

Agenda 21 also backs up my view when it states, 'the structure of power generation will not change fundamentally in the next few years. Assumptions for Poland's energy policy to the year 2010 do not anticipate a significant decline in the role of energy production.'

# POSTSCRIPT

## The Future of Poland

Poland is a large poor country. It is not just her environment that is not up to Western standards. It is her education, health, housing, roads, and social security. In other words, her standard of living. It is a big decision for Western Europe to allow Poland into her Rich Man's Club. Poland's population exceeds that of all the other applicant countries in the first membership tranche put together. Thus the two questions for Brussels 'Should we enlarge the EU eastward?' and 'Should we include Poland?' are nearly the same question, as without Poland there would be no real enlargement. Romania has the next highest population but it is not in the first tranche.

Having decided that eastward enlargement is desirable, and having realised that the price of Polish accession exceeds anything hitherto experienced by member states, it would seem sensible to be most flexible about the conditions of the *Acquis*. There are many chapters in it that will only affect Poles. These concern, for instance, drinking water, health and safety at work, housing and in particular, farming.

Trestour stated 'The *Acquis* is a body of law which can be added to but not altered'.

Does this still hold good? I suggest that there will be many parts of the *Acquis* which the Poles will not be required to implement, and that these will be the parts that affect Poles only and do not affect other countries. Should the European Union insist on the full package there is a danger that it might bankrupt not just Poland, but itself.

There are strong political reasons for admitting Poland to the Union. The cold war only ended 11 years ago and I fear a resurrection of Russian Imperialism. It could come under the guise of a pan Slavic Union.

Meanwhile, Poland may be poor, but it is doing well. It is one of the tiger economies.

We would do well to admit her and we would do well also to respect her conditions of membership. It is not surprising that many Poles regard the West as patronising and even exploitative.

When Poland states that she will not go to Brussels on bended knee, or that she has come away bloodied but unbowed, she is merely echoing the many disappointments that she has experienced in her dealings with the West over the centuries.

Poland deserves our support.

# Acknowledgements

The Author would like to thank the following for their great help in the writing of this book:

Adam, Dr Gordon. MEP.

Adamczyk, Robert. Head of Environmental Department, W.S. Atkins, Warsaw.

Adamiec, Jolanta. Delegation of the European Commission in Poland.

Antonczyk, Jan. Marketing Director, Energoprojekt, Katowice.

Banaszak, Leszek. Deputy Director, Ministry of the Economy, Department of Energy.

Bell, John. Directorate General 1A, Enlarge, European Commission, Brussels.

Bicki, Zbigniew. Former Director of the Polish National Grid.

Biegesz, Boguslaw. Operation Control Manager Rybnik power station.

Borkowski, Zygmunt. Hard Coal Restructuring Agency.

Brach, Andrzej. Vice President Polish Oil and Gas Company.

Bramwell, Anna. Directorate General XI, Environment, Brussels.

Brandt, Jacek. Director of Gielda Energii SA (The Energy Exchange, Warsaw).

Cabal, Vicente Luque. Solid Fuels Unit, DG XVII, Energy, European Commission, Brussels.

Chachlowski, Artur. Huta Sendzimira SA, Krakow.

Chmiel, Andrzej. Financial Counsellor, Polish Embassy, London.

Coey, Marina. Polish National Energy Conservation Agency, Warsaw.

Czarzasty, Edward. Manager, Belchatow power station.

Davies, Michael. Allen and Overy, Warsaw.

Drezewski, Jacek. Managing Director, Krakow CHP (Leg).

Duda, Dr Miroslaw. Bechtel. Adviser to the President of the National Grid.

Ebro-Prokesz. Chief of Management, Krakow CHP (Leg).

Economist Intelligence Unit, The.

Fells, Professor Ian. Fellow, Newcastle University.

Fergusson, Kenneth J. Chief Executive, the Coal Authority, Mansfield, Nottingham.

Fryc, Edward. Vice President and head of project division, Energotechnika, Silesia.

Gawlik, Lydia. Polish Academy of Sciences, Krakow.

Gorlich, Krzysztof. Deputy Mayor of Krakow.

Gorski, Tomasz. Chief Engineer, Investment, Rybnik power station.

Gula, Adam. Director of the Polish Foundation for Energy Efficiency, Krakow.

Green, David, MBE. Director of the Combined Heat and Power Association.

Guyot, Christian. Commercial Director Krakow CHP (Leg).

Herezniak, Wlodzimierz. Director, Weglozbyt SA. Katowice.

Hoscilowicz, Andrzej. Director, New Ventures, Polish Oil and Gas Company.

Hancock, Ewa. Communities section editor 'The Warsaw Voice'.

Jaskiewicz, Jacek. Adviser to the Minister of Environmental Protection.

Juchniewicz, Leszek. President of the Energy Regulatory Authority.

Kaczarewski, Tadeusz. Director, Turow.

Kassenberg, Dr Andrzej. President of the Institute of Sustainable Development, Warsaw.

Kavognchyk, Artur. Jesus College, Oxford.

Kempski, Marek. The Voivod of Silesia.

Kind, Peter. Director, Quality of Life. DG XII. EU Commission, Brussels.

Kobus, Dariusz. Project Manager of PHARE Black Triangle Unit, Czech Republic.

Kowalski, Andrzej. Managing Director Energoprojekt, Katowice SA.

Kowalski, Wojciech. Director, Elektron Consulting.

Kozlowski, Jozef. Economics Director, Turow.

Kozerski, Piotr. Minister Plenipotentiary, Polish Embassy, London.

Krawet, Wieslaw. Vice President Energotechnika Projekt, Silesia.

Kulczycki, Jerzy. Orbis Books, London.

Kurp, Jan. President and Director, Jaworzno III power station.

Lapinski, Ireneusz. General Manager, Skawina power station.

Lizak, Tomasz. Management Board's Office, Belchatow II power station.

Macgregor, M.J., CVO. H.M. Ambassador to Poland.

MacKerron, Gordon. Head of Energy Programme, SPRU. University of Sussex.

Markowski, Dr Jerzy. Senator, Poland.

Mazalerat, Jean Michel. New E de F President of CHP Station Krakow (Leg).

Mayhew, Dr Alan. Head of East European Studies, University of Sussex.

Mazur, Czeslaw. President Energotechnika, Silesia.

Miller, Jerzy. Vice Voivod of Krakow Region.

Najgebauer, Edward. Managing Director, Belchatow power station.

Nikodemski, Marek. Deputy Managing Director Energoprojekt Katowice SA.

Noras, Lucjan. President Weglozbyt SA. Katowice.

Nowok, Pawel. Member of the Sejm (Halemba).

Olbrycht, Jan. Marshal of the Voivodship of Silesia.

Olszowski, Janusz. President, Chamber of Commerce, Katowice.

Orkisz, Zbigniew. Risk Management Department, The Polish Power Grid (PSE).

Parker, Mike. Hon Fellow, SPRU, University of Sussex.

Patterson, Walt. The Royal Institute for International Affairs, Chatham House.

Pattison, Stephen. Director of Trade Promotion, British Embassy, Warsaw.

Pekala, Jozef. President of Opole power station.

Pelczynski, Dr Z.A., OBE. Fellow of Pembroke College, Oxford.

Prior, Mike. Coal specialist. Ian Pope Associates Ltd, Edinburgh.

Sadownik, Adam. Office for the Committee for European Integration, Warsaw.

Schellekens, Pierre. The Polish Desk Officer in DG XI, Environment, Brussels.

Sitko, Franciszek. Director, Halemba Mine.

Smolec, Zygmunt. Director, Agency for the restructuring of the hard coal industry.

Sopicki, Tadeusz. General Manager, Rybnik power station.

Stachowiak-Kowalska, Barbara. Director British/Polish Chamber of Commerce.

Stewart-Clark, Sir Jack. Former Vice President of the European Parliament.

Stretton, Alan. Honorary British Consul Katowice.

Swiebocka, Anna. Office of the Committee for European Integration.

Swierz, Adam. Vice President, District Heating Enterprise, Krakow.

Szablewski, Dr Andrzej. Adviser to the Regulator.

Szczerbiak, Aleks. Lecturer in Polish Political Parties at the University of Sussex.

Szlazak, Dr Jan. Undersecretary of State for Mines, 1999.

Szymanski, Marian. Environmental Protection Specialist, Turow.

Tabis, Wojciech. Director, Department of Energy in Ministry of Economy, Warsaw.

Taylor, Hugh. First Secretary (Commercial) British Embassy, Warsaw.

Tkacz, Anatol. Vice President, Polish Oil and Gas Company.

Trestour, Jean. Chef d'Unite, DGIA (Enlarge) until 1999.

Trybala, Tadeusz. Chief engineer, Turow power station.

Tymowski, Henryk. President of Laziska Power Plant.

Wasiluk-Hassa, Magdalena. Strategy Manager, Polish Power Grid Company.

Walz, Dr Rainer. Deputy Head of Environmental Technology, Karlsruhe University.

Watson, Dr Jim. SPRU. University of Sussex.

Wertz, Jerzy. Environment protection department. Office of Voivod in Krakow.

Wesolowski, Ireneusz. Deputy Technical Director, Opole power station.

Winiarski, Witold. Director, Chamber of Commerce, Katowice.

Winnicki, Leszek. Director, Opole power station.

Wojcik, Darius. Jesus College, Oxford.

Wolinski, Jacek. Executive Director, Huta Sendzimira.

Woloch, Marek. President of Tadeusz Kosciuszko Polaniec power station.

World Coal Institute, The, Upper Richmond Rd, London.

Wozny, Przemyslaw. Assistant Director, Belchatow power station.

Wroblewska, Elzbieta. Principal specialist, Department of Energy.

Zagala, Janusz. Vice President of Grupa Energotechnika.

Zaleski, Boguslaw. Director of the Energy Regulatory Authority.

Zerka, Marek. Director of corporate strategy, Polish Power Grid Co.

Zmijewski, Krzysztof. President of the Polish Power Grid (PSE).

# Index

## A

Adam, Dr Gordon  168
Agenda 2000  177, 181, 184
Agenda 21  196
Ahaus  153
ALTENER  170
Anderson, Kym  67
Apache  77
Auschwitz  18
AWS Party  36,  37,  38

## B

Balcerowicz, Leszek  30, 31, 35 - 37,
   39,  41,  66, 160, 162,  194,  195
Barnett, Lord  167
Battle, John  143
Belchatow  **88**,  184
Bicki, Zbigniew  113
Bielecki  28
Birt, John  23
black triangle  91
Blue Circle Cement  66
Bogdanka  48,  105
'Bolek'  29
Brandt, Jacek  117
Brotherhood Pipeline  73
Budge, Richard J.  65, 139, 172, 193
Buggenum  132
Buk, Halima  71
Bush, George  85
Buzek, Jerzy  24, 36
Bytom  57,  58

## C

Cabal, Vicente Luque  135,  145
Ceausescu  26
CEEBIC  115, 117

CENTREL  104
Chernobyl  19
Cimoszewicz  35,  36
Coey, Marina  127
Contracts for Difference  142
Copenhagen  Conference  162
Corus  44
Czysta Polska  68

## D

Davies, Michael  98,  181,  193
Drax  187
Drinking Water Directive  183
DTI  139,  141
Duda, Dr Miroslaw  77,  118

## E

EBRD  53,  119,  165,  166, 169
EIB  170
EKOFUND  127
Ekopal  68
Electricité de France  72, 103,  172
Elektrim  95
Endesa  107
Energoprojekt of Katowice  134
Energy Exchange see Gielda
Energy Law  111
Energy Restructuring Group  163
Enron  140
ESCOs  127,  170
European Council  161,  162

## F

Favrat, Elizabeth  121
Fluidised beds  130
Foster Wheeler  93,  94

## G

gas, Norwegian 76
gas, Russian 45
Gasunie 83
Gazprom 76, 150
Gielda (Energy Exchange) 115, 117
Gierek 22
Global Environmental Facility 84
Gomulka 16, 22
Gorbachev 23
Gorleben 153
Green, David 70
Gula, Dr Adam 86, 104, 127

## H

Haslam, Lord 109
Havel, Vaclav 27
Heseltine, Michael 139
Hoening 70
Hughes, Kirsty 189
Huta Katowice 17, 44, 45

## I

IGCC 132
Integrated Prevention of Pollution
  Control Directive (IPPC) 183
International Monetary Fund 32

## J

Jaruzelski 23, 25, 26
Jaworzno III **108**
JOULE-THERMIE 170
Juchniewicz, Leszek 76, 84, 90, 94,
  103, 110, 112-118, 121, 180, 194 - 195

## K

KAPE 127
Kassenberg, Professor Andrzej 86
Kohlepfennig 154, 155
Kolodziej, Piotr 71
Kozlowski, Josef 93, 94
Krzazklewski 36
Kurp, Jan 108

Kwasniewski 35, 36, 37, 194
Kyoto 42, 54, 116, 139, 149, 152

## L

Large Combustion Plant Directive
  (LCPD) 182, 183, 187
Laziska **109**
Leg CHP 72
Littlechild, Stephen 142, 143
Lublin 48, 105

## M

MacCarthy, Callum 143
Madrid Conference 162
Markowski, Dr Jerzy 54, 55, 65, 69
Marshall, Walter 137
Mayhew, Alan 167
Mazalerat, Jean Michel 72
Mazowiecki 26, 28
McDowall CBE, John 44
Millard, Frances 31, 39
Ministry of Mines 19
Mossadeq 136

## N

Najgebauer, Edward 90
Neisse River 18
neo-Communists (SLD) 34
Netherlands Energy Research
  Foundation 169
Noras, Lucjan 46
Northern Lights Pipeline 73
Nowa Huta 17
Nowa Sarzyna (Enron) 78

## O

Oder River 18
OECD 32
Olbrycht, Jan 44
Oleksy 35
Olszewski, Jan 29, 32
Olszewski plan 48
Opole **107**

**P**

Patnow-Adamov-Konin **88**, 193
Pawlak 29, 34, 35
Peasants' Party 34, 37
Pekala, Josef 107
POGC 74 - 77
Polaniec **105**, 118, 193
Polish Department of Energy 57
Pool, The 142
Price Waterhouse 57
Prugar, Wieslaw 75, 76
Prus, Aleksandra 57
PSL Party 34

**R**

RJB Mining see Budge, Richard J.
Ruhrgas 149, 150
Ruhrgasindustrie 149
Rybnik **106**, 118

**S**

Sachs, Jeffrey 30
Samecki, Pawel 167
SAVE 170
Scargill, Arthur 138
Schröder 146, 148
Scierski, Klemens 101
Second Sulphur Protocol 111
Sellafield 153
Siersza 57
Single Buyer 174
SLD 34, 36, 37
Slocock 120, 121
Small Combustion Plant
  Directive 191
Smolec, Zygmunt 48, 58, 59
Solidarity 22, 26, 28, 34
Solidarity Electoral Action 36
Sopicki, Tadeusz 106
Suchocka, Hanna 29
SYNERGY 170
Synergy Poland 47, 175, 176, 178
System Marginal Price 142
Szlazak, Jan 46, 61, 108, 195

**T**

Tatra mountains 86
Torrens, Ian (Shell) 133
TPA, negotiated 173
    regulated 173
Tractabel 105
Treblinka 18
Trestour, Jean 108
Turow **88**

**U**

UCPTE 104
Urban Waste Water Directive 183
Usti 93, 169

**V**

Vattenfall 117
Versailles, Treaty of 15
Vistula River 20, 36

**W**

Walesa, Lech 22, 26, 28, 29, 35, 36
Watson, Jim 133
Weglokoks 61, 64
Weglozbyt 46
Wierzchowice 79
Wingas 150
Winskel 137
Wojtyla, Cardinal Karol
  (the Pope) 23
Woloch, Marek 105
World Bank 32, 53, 56, 165, 166, 169

**Y**

Yamal 80, 83, 150

**Z**

Zamosc (CHP) 78
Zarnowiec 78, 86
Zerka, Marek 113
Zmijewski 110, 113, 114, 118, 195
Zomo (Police) 23